The
Farthest
Shore

The
Farthest
Shore

Seeking solitude and nature on
the Cape Wrath Trail in winter

ALEX RODDIE

Vertebrate Publishing, Sheffield
www.v-publishing.co.uk

The
Farthest
Shore

ALEX RODDIE

First published in 2021 by Vertebrate Publishing.

 Vertebrate Publishing
Omega Court, 352 Cemetery Road, Sheffield S11 8FT, United Kingdom.
www.v-publishing.co.uk

This book is a work of non-fiction. The author has stated to the publishers that, except in such minor respects not affecting the substantial accuracy of the work, the contents of the book are true.

A CIP catalogue record for this book is available from the British Library.

ISBN: 978-1-83981-020-6 (Paperback)
ISBN: 978-1-83981-021-3 (Ebook)
ISBN: 978-1-83981-022-0 (Audiobook)

10 9 8 7 6 5 4 3 2 1

Cover design by Jane Beagley, Vertebrate Publishing.
Production by Rosie Edwards, Vertebrate Publishing.
www.v-publishing.co.uk

Vertebrate Publishing is committed to printing on paper from sustainable sources.

Printed and bound in the UK by TJ Books Limited, Padstow, Cornwall.

In memory of Ian Roddie,
1938–2018

Contents

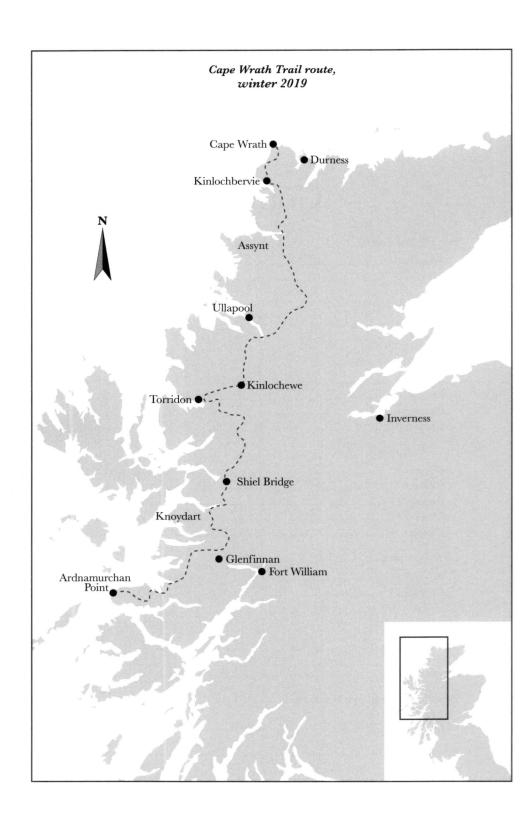

Cape Wrath Trail route,
winter 2019

N

Cape Wrath
Durness
Kinlochbervie

Assynt

Ullapool

Kinlochewe
Torridon

Inverness

Shiel Bridge

Knoydart

Glenfinnan
Fort William

Ardnamurchan
Point

Only in silence the word,
Only in dark the light,
Only in dying life:
Bright the hawk's flight
On the empty sky.

—Ursula K. Le Guin, from *A Wizard of Earthsea*

PART 1

Enmeshment

Chapter 1

December 2018, Knoydart, Scottish Highlands

I'd come to this high, wild and lonely place to escape from my anxiety for a while, but it had followed me here like a dog.

Ever since entering Knoydart the day before, the menace of a missing bridge had hung over me like a rotten branch, for the old bridge over the River Carnach had been the key to getting through this rugged country by the well-trodden routes. But the bridge was gone. Floods the year before had obliterated it, and now the river surged dark and deep from a source high in the mountains to outflow in Loch Nevis, drawing a line through the ambitions of wanderers in these mountains. So, afraid of a bridgeless river crossing that had killed walkers before, I had scoured my map for alternatives. Precious few leapt out at me. Each would be, in winter at least, as formidable in its own way as the river crossing.

At Corryhully bothy two nights before, I'd chatted with a hillwalker who had been making forays into Knoydart to pick off a few of the Munros. His surprise when I'd trudged in out of the cold night had been palpable.

'Not many come here in December,' he'd said an hour or two later, after whisky and firelight had softened the stranger-caution between us, as these things do in bothies. 'It's my favourite time of year now,' he added a moment later. 'Years ago it was always like this – quiet, like. Now it's busy here during the summer. I blame the Cape Wrath Trail.'

I nodded. 'I'll be back to do the whole CWT in February. For now I'm just checking out the route through Knoydart, to see how it goes in winter.' My pause felt uneasy. 'There's a bridge missing.'

I couldn't articulate the complex flutter of guilt that came to me then – the knowledge, so recently awakened in me, that my own published writing had contributed to the trail's popularity since I had first hiked it four years before – and so I said nothing, letting the sting of cowardice feed the new, outdoorsy kind of anxiety I was carrying around with me these days.

The Cape Wrath Trail is commonly cited as the UK's wildest and most difficult long-distance hike, extending for around 400 kilometres from Fort William to Cape Wrath, the northwesternmost point of the British mainland. There is no official CWT; many variant routes exist, some more difficult than others. The trail is not waymarked and there is frequently no path underfoot. There are unbridged rivers to cross, bogs to negotiate, big distances to cover between possible resupply locations. This puts the trail a cut above more popular Scottish backpacking routes such as the West Highland Way. Aspirant CWT hikers need to be tough, experienced, and competent navigators over rough ground. Yet, despite all this, the trail has become significantly more popular in recent years, partly thanks to me and a few other outdoor writers. I still didn't know quite how I felt about this. Writing about the Cape Wrath Trail had helped to launch my own career as an outdoor writer, but I wondered what impact I'd had on a fragile environment – and on the ineffable sense of solitude and remoteness to be found there.

My pal saw none of this. His eyes had widened when I'd mentioned coming back to do the CWT in February, and he nodded at my mention of the bridge. 'The Carnach can be a bastard of a crossing when the river's high. How are you getting around it, then?'

I told him my plans, and he wished me luck, and the next day I ventured out into the quiet snowless early winter glow of Knoydart.

For reasons I couldn't explain then, so much seemed to depend on this – on my plans for a winter Cape Wrath Trail, and therefore on my reconnaissance trip. Something had been building within me for months. Or perhaps draining out of me. There were times when it was easy to tell myself that it wasn't real: when laughing about something silly with Hannah, when caught up in that godlike flow of writing something meaningful, when immersed in nature high on a hill with the humming galaxies of the internet far from my mind. Especially that last one. Time in nature nurtured me – except, increasingly it seemed, when it didn't.

Bealach Coire nan Gall. I'd read the place name on my map of Knoydart, but I didn't know how to pronounce it. There was no path leading over this 733-metre saddle between two mountains, but the contours hadn't looked too bad, and I'd guessed that I could walk over this col. It would be my way to avoid the missing bridge. Getting to this high point had been a classic Knoydart slog: squelch, splash, squelch for a couple of hours up a steep slope of deer grass and moss, wandering back and forth to avoid rock outcrops on my way. Fortunately, or perhaps unfortunately, there was no snow on the ground. The coppery texture of what sparse vegetation could withstand the deer showed everywhere, leaving me to imagine how different – how much sketchier – this ascent would be under heavy snow, as it could easily be on my next visit in February for the real deal.

It'll be fine, I told myself as the angle steepened yet again and I visualised this slope cloaked in a soggy, avalanche-prone layer of snow. *It had better bloody be.* I found myself idly wondering which would be worse – to be swept off my feet by a river in spate, dragged under freezing water by a heavy winter pack, or to be avalanched in a place like this and rolled hundreds of metres downhill to a silent burial until spring. Not much of a choice.

The climb levelled out and I picked my way across an area of black crags that sprouted from knolls and hillocks. I could hear a raven up there somewhere, croaking at me. I tripped over something hard and looked down to see a finger of old tree root poking out of the peat, its surface encrusted with grey-green lichen. It may have been hundreds or even thousands of years old, a relic of ancient woodlands now long gone, cleared by humans and kept locked deep in the soil by the deer. Ahead of me lay one final, brief climb to the bealach, and then at last I'd get a look at what lay on the other side.

The north wind blasted me in a sudden fury as I reached the highest point, and I staggered back a step, bracing with my trekking poles.

Clouds the colour of hammered tin ripped over the mountains to the north. The thread of a river led my eye in that direction, into the heart of Knoydart – this strange, sad and beautiful land that had once been a home to hundreds of people, centuries ago. It was a working landscape still, but a depopulated one. Echoes of Knoydart's sadness reached me sometimes when I trod its old paths, but at that moment, cheeks raw from the northern blast, I felt nothing but a fierce and primal joy. My instinct had been correct. There was a way through into the inner realm. Steep ground dropped away on the other side of the bealach; it wouldn't be easy under snow, but it would go. I felt a little like I imagined an eagle might feel when cresting a new ridgeline on a thermal.

Then, piercing through the moment like a knife, I felt a familiar tidal tug from somewhere deep in my brain stem: the impulse to take a photo on my phone and stick it up on social media. The impulse to validate this feeling of primordial success and make it real. If you climb a mountain but don't Instagram the view from the summit, have you even climbed it? I wanted the answer to be yes – knew it to be – but, somehow, incredibly, I didn't always believe it. I let the impulse crash over me, hating it, and ignored the twitch for my phone. There was no signal anyway. Knoydart was a big, glorious blackspot as far as mobile signal was concerned. That's why I'd come, but although my disconnection was absolute, my solitude as pristine as it could be, I didn't feel as if I'd broken free from the internet and its insistent, jittery demands on my time and attention after all.

Chapter 2

January 2018 (eleven months earlier), Pilgrim Hospital, Lincolnshire

'The Russian doc says it's an infection in my leg. On top of the lymphoma, of course.'

Dad's tone was gentle, quiet, upbeat, as it always was whenever he found himself back on Ward 7a. A grey T-shirt and blue chequered pyjama bottoms hung over his thinning frame. The tube from a cannula curled from his arm to a machine on a stand beside the bed. My dad had never had much meat on him, but now I could see the bones quite clearly – the defined outline of cranium straining through papery, mottled skin beneath a wisp of white hair. It had never grown back quite right since his spell in remission, and I was still getting used to this new version of Ian Roddie, with slightly roguish tufts growing above his ears.

'Another infection,' Mum said from where she was sitting at the bedside, just in front of me.

She had not taken off her large green fleece, despite the heat of the ward. The bright lights reflected off her glasses. She was looking intently at Dad and seemed to have forgotten that Hannah and I were sitting just behind her on those blue chairs that ward visitors always had to fight over at this time in the evening.

'Antibiotics again,' Dad said, and when he looked away from Mum and smiled at me I saw unfathomable emotions in the wells of his eyes – an expression that touched the core of me, although I couldn't name it.

Sitting beside me, Hannah had rested a hand on my knee and was stroking it absently. I found the gesture soothing, but it didn't stop my thoughts from anxiously flip-flopping as Mum and Dad's conversation moved to safer topics such as the weather – 'The nurses have told me there's a foot of snow on its way' – to everyone's favourite topic, the upcoming Roddie wedding – 'Have you been back to the venue yet? Any thoughts about your flowers?' This drew a smile, as always, because Hannah is a professional florist who had known precisely what kind of flowers she wanted for years. Probably before I even asked her to marry me. I dropped in comments here and there, but could think of nothing real to say. Suddenly the ticking of the clock on the wall seemed incredibly loud, and all I could see in that room were the wires and the screens and the sensors. The image returned to me, again, of the invisible structure of cables and software and emails, always emails, that in some abstract and awful way functioned as my own life-support system.

Emails never stopped. Months ago I'd deleted the app from my phone, and that worked for a while, but they were always stacking up in the background out of sight, weren't they? I could never escape from them. They would always need to be assessed and sorted and replied to and deleted. I knew that I was good at my job, responsive to communication, but sometimes I found it hard to deal with on top of everything else – a tyrannical presence that eroded my boundaries between work and life. The remote worker's curse? The curse of the millennial freelance creative, or whatever they were calling us now? Even at that moment, when my dad was trying to talk to his family and show in his mild way what living with non-Hodgkin's lymphoma was really like, the weight of all those emails was accumulating in my mind. A relentless task list set for me by distant people who didn't know about any of this messy horror out here beyond the internet, in the besieged corners of my life I so often failed to prevent being overrun by work.

We said our goodbyes at leaving time and promised, as we did every day, that we'd see Dad tomorrow. Mum got up from her chair and kissed him on the forehead.

'No dancing,' she said with a small laugh as she always did.

Dad reached up, his bare arm brutalised by cannulas and the bruised places where they'd failed to get cannulas in so many times, the fragile skin looking like some kind of battleground, and gripped her own arm for a moment as they said goodbye. His expression looked mischievous, impish, despite the hollow cheeks and exhaustion. In a strange and tragic way this long illness had brought us all closer together. But I also knew that he was haunted by a terrible fear, one that nobody dared name: that he would not live long enough to be there at our wedding in May.

As we rose to leave, a young nurse in a white uniform whirled in with her trolley of medicines and gizmos. 'Evening, Ian!' she said with a bright smile, after a more subdued smile in our direction. 'You look wonderful today, Ian.'

'I wish I didn't feel wonderful,' Dad said with a chuckle, then looked at me again with that expression I cannot describe.

On our way across the car park, I felt Hannah's small, cold hand slip into mine. I turned to her. The lights from the hospital, a vast monolith behind us, made her copper hair glow like a ragged halo, but her eyes were dark. And as I helped Mum back into the car, neither of us saying anything for once, I felt the dreadful compulsion to check for notifications on my phone.

*****

A week later

That week, I'd felt a desire to go back to Glen Coe so powerful it had scared me a little. The threads of an old life were there – old friends, old adventures, surrounded by the mountains I loved. It had been too long since my last real trip to the hills. I found myself daydreaming about the perfect snowy wild camp I'd enjoy in the Lost Valley, followed by a climb on the steep ice of Bidean nam Bian's north face, ice axe and crampons biting flawless *névé* just like in the old days, followed by a long ridge walk and descent back to the Clachaig Inn where a pint of Nessie's Monster Mash and a plate of haggis would be waiting for me. This plan, which was not really a plan at all but a wish marbled with old memories, would be my escape from the cruelty of cancer for a few days.

When I'd told Dad about my planned trip on a visit one night, that expression had illuminated his eyes again – love, I thought, blended with acceptance but also a consuming regret. And that night, at home in bed with Hannah, she held me tightly and I whispered to her, 'I can't go. I know he seems basically fine at the moment, but I can't. Something awful is going to happen if I go to Scotland.'

She kissed me and said, 'Aren't they sending him home? I thought they were fairly happy with the infection.'

I shook my head but said nothing. Yes, they were sending him home, but I knew what I'd seen in his eyes. We'd been here many times before – this was not the first infection to have stalled treatment. But it felt different this time. *He knew.*

Four days later, after a brief final spell at home, Dad was back in hospital again. He'd fallen out of bed in the middle of the night and Mum had found him weak, floppy and confused. The infection was back. After the ambulance had taken him to Ward 7a, we heard the word 'sepsis'.

A few days after that, Mum got a call at about ten o'clock in the morning advising us all to come in right away.

The vigil began. My brother James and his partner Nicole were hurrying down from Scotland. After a while, when a bed became available, the nurses moved Dad from the shared ward to a private room. It had been too intense, clustered around the bedside with the curtains drawn and Dad fighting for breath through the drugs, other patients and other visitors an arm's length away. Things felt calmer in the subdued light of the private room – the one, I realised, he'd occupied when first hospitalised for cancer back in 2016. They upgraded his drugs and he calmed down, but a little more of the life faded out of him.

After the tears and confusion, after the questions and halting half-answers, after several of the nurses had asked to come in to hold his hand for a moment and say goodbye, there came the waiting. Hannah was crocheting something out of green wool; Mum was reading a novel; I stared into space.

The waiting continued. We stayed there that night, Hannah and I dozing on uncomfortable chairs in the visitors' room while Mum kept watch at the bedside. Starlings woke me with their chattering outside the window before dawn. James texted me to say they'd been held up by the snow and wouldn't arrive for some hours yet. When morning came, Dad was still breathing deeply and peacefully, as if in defiance of the doctor's euphemistic 'I'm afraid I should warn you that he is *very poorly* this time.'

At about ten o'clock that morning, I found myself alone with my dad for a while. James and Nicole were still an hour or more away, and Hannah had driven Mum back to her house to pick up a change of clothes and a few other things. So I sat at the bedside and watched my dying father. His arms didn't look as if they belonged to him any more. They had often been swollen during his long illness, but never as swollen as this. Between the bruises, the skin looked dry, yellowing and flaky. Occasionally he shifted or twitched, but his arms never moved – dead weights, as if the spark of his life had already retreated from those extremities.

After a while, I put on the radio. BBC Radio 3 was playing a morning concert: one of the Mozart symphonies. Dad's favourite music, and some of mine too. I smiled and turned up the volume. Thin winter sunlight had begun to stream in through the window and suddenly there was a feeling of spring here in this room – perhaps because Mozart, to me, always felt like long May afternoons in the garden at our old house in Caxton, where we'd lived when I was a child, with Dad building something in his shed and one of his Mozart tapes playing on the ancient tape deck he kept there. There would always be the rhythmic *ca-coooo-coo-coo* of a wood pigeon in the background. The smile bubbled up in me, unstoppable.

My pocket buzzed with a text message. As I reached for my phone to read it – James was only twenty minutes away now – I realised, startled, that apart from texting James I had not looked at my phone the whole time we'd been at the hospital. I hadn't felt the compulsion to listlessly scroll through Twitter, or update myself on whatever dystopian headlines were all over the news. The urge hadn't even been there. And, blissfully, I realised that I had stopped subconsciously tallying up the emails I knew would be waiting for me when I got home too. There was just silence. A poignant, almost nostalgic solitude, just me and my dad.

To break this moment by losing myself to the no-time of Twitter, even for an instant, would feel like a crime.

'Do you remember—' I began, then stopped. He couldn't hear me. Or could he? 'Do you remember all the stories you used to tell me and James about your old life on the boat in Suffolk? About *Yorrel?* I was always fascinated by the idea of you living out there on the river by yourself for days at a time, back in the seventies. I always loved the sound of that isolation.'

As the music played, and as Mozart moved on to Vivaldi, I started telling some of those stories back to him. About winters on the River Deben so fierce that the estuary partially froze. About starlight and sunsets, and the warbling music of a thousand curlews over the marshes – a music that, thanks to climate change and biodiversity loss, was diminished now. I told him about a dawn of such perfect stillness that the vast waters became a mirror, reflecting back the reds and purples of the sky in a way that he would remember for forty years; that most silent and beautiful sunrise on an otherwise unremarkable day in April, distinguished only by the fact that nobody else was on the river to see it. The spectacle was his alone to witness.

As I told those stories back to him, I couldn't help but feel a sense of loss. Not only would I never hear my dad tell me those tales again himself, but they came from a world that no longer even existed. In the 1970s, to go and spend the night on a boat on the river was to disconnect. My dad could not have been pestered by work demands or the Pavlovian urge to look at social media, to let the world's voices in for a while, drowning out his own inner voice with a thousand new things to get excited or upset about or form an opinion on. The technology simply didn't exist. But everyone had a mobile phone now. With a jolt, I realised that even my dad, the ultimate smartphone refusenik, would not have been able to achieve pristine solitude on the river in the present day unless he kept his basic phone switched off, which he no doubt would. Even then, the potential for connection would remain. Perhaps, I thought, along with everything we've gained, we've also lost something: the ability to be truly, unequivocally alone with our own thoughts on our own terms.

I thought back to my own last solitary experience of a wild and beautiful place. In July I'd walked 200 miles through the forests of Norway, and I'd taken my phone and my headphones. Audiobooks and quick hits of validation from posting photos to Instagram had kept me entertained. Most of the trail had bathed in strong 4G signal. I could remember plenty of scenes of natural beauty, but at that moment, compared to the experience my dad had enjoyed decades ago, no doubt intensified by the emotions of this moment and the power of repeated storytelling, my own recollections from Norway seemed distant and faded. Nothing unique or special about them at all. Just a big walk in the woods. Had I even noticed or observed anything? Or had I been so preoccupied that the chance for genuine solitude, and the openness, the attentiveness it might bring, had been lost? What have we done to our experience of being outdoors?

My dad shifted and made a noise in the back of his throat. I was convinced that he had heard my words. His breathing was easier now. Of all the things he had taught me during his life, perhaps this – something I already half-knew, but had never considered in these terms – was one of the most important. Had I given something back to him in those final hours, painting images of sunsets and stillness in his mind?

I said a few more things that needed to be said. Vivaldi moved on to Beethoven. James and Nicole burst into the ward; in her face I read relief that their delayed journey hadn't cost them the chance for a final goodbye, and in his I saw a suppressed pain. James looked thin again and I thought I saw lines spreading from the corners of his eyes. I wondered how he was coping, if the domineering presence of his depression were making itself felt again. Now was not the time. Soon, Mum and Hannah came back. Hannah hugged me fiercely, and in her wordless glance we communicated more than could be said. She had lost her father too. The next bit was going to be hard.

It was. But we were all there, and I never forgot that final precious hour alone with my dad, telling stories and listening to music – a seminar on the gifts of solitude, faced with the imminent prospect of that final and ultimate solitude.

***

I've always known that I can't think properly when my mind is jacked in to the internet, but only in the last few years have I thought to ask why.

It started when I was studying for my degree in Computing Science at the University of East Anglia, Norwich. I began my studies in 2005, a few years before a double-whammy digital revolution: social media and smartphones. Back then, there were plenty of ways to waste time on the internet, but you had to be sitting in front of a computer to do so. That had changed by the time I graduated in 2008. Facebook, which I'd joined in July 2006 when it was for university students only, opened up to the general public two months later. Mobile phones had become far more sophisticated in a short period of time, and although it would take a while for most people to upgrade to a smartphone, I remember my first sighting of an iPhone in the wild in 2008 and thinking *this is the future.* For the majority of my degree course, though, the internet was something you accessed from a desktop or laptop. Even in that innocent time, it was like a wrecking ball through my attention span and ability to concentrate.

Put yourself in my shoes. I was nineteen years old and living away from home for the first time. I'd always found it difficult to make friends, and now I'd left all my old friends behind, forced to start from scratch. I was overweight and introverted and self-conscious. Everyone else seemed to be going out to parties and having fun, but I felt awkward and out of place at the few hall parties I forced myself to attend in those first couple of months at uni. My attempts to fit in were painful. Early on, I'd realised that my preference for classical music wouldn't make me many friends, so I'd pretended to enjoy rock instead. It didn't work. Invariably, I found myself stuck at home, browsing hillwalking or writing forums while other students on my floor were going out to the pub.

Internet forums let me be myself. They provided social validation and the company of like-minded individuals. I didn't have to pretend to like Van Halen when I was posting on Outdoors Magic or the Forward Motion writing community. On the internet I had a voice and I felt valued.

This combination proved deadly. I found it increasingly difficult to get off the internet and get on with my work. Partly that was because I needed my computer for my studies, and when compiling Java code in Net-Beans all the distractions of the internet were only a click away. I became a master procrastinator, wasting hours on forums and compulsively hitting the refresh key to see if I'd had any replies. Deadlines would creep up on me; more than once, I found myself pulling all-nighters in the library in order to get my work done.

I did make friends at UEA eventually, and by the second year I was living a normal student lifestyle, complete with regular trips to the pub, drunken escapades and the occasional house party. I'd found a tribe of people who didn't care that I preferred Beethoven to Snow Patrol and who appreciated my various quirks. I'd discovered girls too. Although I had started to spend less time online, by this point damaging patterns of behaviour had become firmly established; when faced with a task that required intense concentration, I was unable to resist wasting time on the internet. All my friends were on Facebook by this point. Facebook took previous methods of procrastination and dialled them up to 100, super-charged with new features such as notifications, 'pokes', games, groups and apps. Flicking over to the Facebook tab became a reflexive impulse.

When I eventually upgraded to a smartphone in 2010, Facebook was the first app I installed. I met my future wife Hannah on the UKClimbing forum in the same year, and our relationship blossomed largely thanks to Facebook. In the years after this, I became ever more dependent on social media. In 2014 I started working as a freelance writer and editor, and social media was how I found clients and readers. I'd become more enmeshed with the internet than ever before. And, more than ever before, I found my ability to concentrate on the work that mattered – even, at times, my ability to *think* – fundamentally compromised. By 2012 I found it difficult to sit down with a good book without reflexively reaching for my phone every ten minutes. I wondered what the hell was wrong with me.

For years, I assumed that my own lack of willpower was to blame, that this was my fault. It took me a long time to learn that this wasn't entirely accurate – that subtle forces beyond my control or knowledge had been manipulating me. The fragmentation of attention had become big business, and people had no idea.

In *Utopia is Creepy*, Nicholas Carr writes that 'Distraction is the permanent end state of the perfected consumer, not least because distraction is a state that is eminently programmable.'[1] The first book I read by this author, *The Shallows: How the internet is changing the way we think, read and remember,* was a wake-up call; it reveals how people read in a fundamentally different way online, and presents evidence that the time we spend on the internet may be harming our ability to read and think deeply. I read about how social platforms are designed to be addictive, to make people anxious and upset, to deepen social divisions, because that makes more money for advertisers. In his no-holds-barred treatise against social media called *Ten Arguments for Deleting Your Social Media Accounts Right Now,* Jaron Lanier explains how it works:

> *Customized feeds become optimized to "engage" each user, often with emotionally potent cues, leading to addiction. People don't realize how they are being manipulated. The default purpose of manipulation is to get people more and more glued in, and to get them to spend more and more time in the system.*[2]

As I read more widely, things started to make sense. For me, those 'emotionally potent cues' related at first to social belonging and banishing loneliness, but nobody is immune; human beings are social animals, and we all crave validation. That's why it's incredibly difficult not to look when you see the red notification badge light up in your Facebook app. You want to know what people are saying about you. When a post gets a lot of likes, you feel good – and when it doesn't, you feel ignored, a rollercoaster of emotions that contributes to the addictive nature of social media. The brain chemical at work here is dopamine, sometimes known as the pleasure chemical. Notifications are a bit like a slot machine, and

---

1 Carr, *Utopia is Creepy: And Other Provocations,* 65
2 Lanier, *Ten Arguments for Deleting Your Social Media Accounts Right Now,* 31

the humble 'like' button – now present on every social platform – has been shown to be incredibly addictive.[3]

For the first time, I started to understand how I had been manipulated into spending so much of my time scrolling and liking and sharing. I didn't resent the genuine interactions with family, friends and colleagues, but I did resent all the other stuff: the compulsive checking, the fake news, the flame wars, the trolls, the inability to concentrate on anything, the growing feeling of numbness after I'd spent too long on the internet. The time speeding up and slipping away. It was precious time subtracted from my life – and what did I have to show for it? I also soon realised that there was a gulf between awareness of the problem and actually changing my own behaviour. I experimented with deleting apps from my phone, taking half-hearted breaks from social media, trying to go back to a basic dumbphone for a while. I even stopped using Facebook permanently. Nothing seemed to work. When I left Facebook, I found myself spending more time on Twitter. Same drug, different packaging.

In his book *Digital Minimalism,* computer scientist Cal Newport explains how the invention of the smartphone created a new attack vector for social media to banish whatever solitude once existed in our lives:

> *The smartphone provided a new technique to banish these remaining slivers of solitude:* the quick glance. *At the slightest hint of boredom, you can now surreptitiously glance at any number of apps or mobile-adapted websites that have been optimized to provide you an immediate and satisfying dose of input from other minds.*[4]

Genuine solitude, I realised, had long been absent from my life. With multitudes of real-life friends, old colleagues I no longer really spoke to, and online acquaintances constantly there in an always-on ambient presence on the other side of various screens, I was never actually alone.

---

3 Busby, M., 'Social media copies gambling methods "to create psychological cravings"', *The Guardian* (published online 8 May 2018), https://www.theguardian.com/technology/2018/may/08/social-media-copies-gambling-methods-to-create-psychological-cravings

4 Newport, *Digital Minimalism: On Living Better with Less Technology,* 101

I would tweet a thought before taking the time to reflect on it, and then it would be gone, a bird fluttering out into cyberspace. What was that doing to me?

By early 2018, work had grown busy and complicated, and the quantity of email I received every day had spiralled out of control. The stress caused by my dad's long illness and death compounded everything else, adding to the overwhelm I felt. Before, my reaction to too much time online had felt like a buzzing, grey emptiness; now it felt more like red panic, and yet I was so hopelessly entangled that I still couldn't look away. When I opened my email account, I felt crushed, stupefied, burnt out. When I logged in to Twitter, I saw dystopian headlines and political division, and yet Twitter was where I found new clients, found readers for my work, made genuine connections. I wrote in my diary that I was heading towards a nervous breakdown. Something had to change.

I would fantasise about stepping away from the internet entirely. I read about 'Walden Zones': offline cabins or retreats where internet access was impossible and people could achieve zen-like focus alone with their own thoughts. I remembered the writing shed I'd once had at the bottom of the garden at my parents' house in Suffolk. In those days, before uni, I could rattle off 3,000 words of awful prose an hour with no internet to distract me. Such productivity was unimaginable fifteen years later, when I'd struggle with a blank text document for half a day, anxiously watching emails pinging into my inbox and notifications racking up in a Twitter window in the background. Even when I managed to escape to my happy place in the mountains, social media followed me there, ruining any chance of genuine solitary reflection or observation in nature.

'The tragedy is that the stroll, the camping trip, and the face-to-face chat are now themselves suffused with digital ephemera,' writes Nicholas Carr. 'Even if we agreed to turn off our gadgets for a spell, they remain ghostly presences.'[5]

I felt those ghostly presences constantly. I had felt them during my dad's illness, and I felt them when offline in the mountains. Was the internet to blame for this change in me, or was it the destruction of solitude

---

5 Carr, *Utopia is Creepy*, 129

that the internet – and my smartphone – had facilitated? Had I just grown up but failed to adapt to my responsibilities? Was my anxiety caused by some other factor altogether? I had no way of telling, and I realised that I needed to get a new perspective on the problem. My disorganised attempts at getting to the bottom of it had all failed. I needed a scorched-earth solution.

***

September 2018

I'd come up with the idea a couple of months before, but didn't find the right time to discuss it with Hannah until we were on our honeymoon in the Scottish Highlands.

'So you'll be completely out of contact?' she said from a little way ahead along the path. She reached up to move a rowan branch out of her way; it splashed her with droplets. 'For an entire month?'

Our honeymoon had been special. We'd got married back in May after almost eight years as a couple. My dad had lived to see us get engaged, but, heartbreakingly, he hadn't lived to see the wedding – in fact, during his last week he'd told us about his dreams of being late to the ceremony, of stopped clocks and locked doors. We'd both had a year of highs and lows. When it came time to plan our Scottish honeymoon, we looked for one thing above all else: peace and quiet. I'd brought no work of any kind with me, looked at no emails and spent a bare minimum of time on social media, just posting a handful of photos for family and friends. Our time and our attention would be for each other, we'd decided – and the strategy had worked. The depth of my relaxation on this trip served to highlight how anxious and on edge I'd been for so long.

But I was looking ahead, and in early 2019 I wanted to break out of the old cycle and do something entirely new. I'd outlined my plan to her as we walked through the silent pines and autumn colours of Anagach Woods near Grantown-on-Spey.

'You want to hike the Cape Wrath Trail again,' my wife was saying to me, and this time she turned so that I could see her smile. 'In winter this time. With no internet at all.'

'Well summarised.' I stepped over a fallen branch thick with lichen. The silence in this wood felt textured, expectant, observant.

'Why?' She drew the word out with a chuckle, and I heard her unspoken subtext: *you always whinge about the weather when you go backpacking in winter, and isn't your recent obsession with being offline just another phase?* Or maybe I was hearing my own insecurities in her voice.

'I think I'll be able to answer that when I've done it. I just know that I have to.'

'OK,' she said, and this time I heard acceptance.

We stopped to admire a red squirrel, leaping from branch to branch in the pines high above. At our own level, a spray of flame-coloured birch leaves caught the light. This forest, diverse and dynamic and full of relatively intact ecosystems, made me feel alive in a way that most don't. Although only a few hundred years old, Anagach Woods felt ancient – a taste of the older, wilder woods we had almost entirely lost, vanished beneath the plough and the grouse moors and the stalking estates. Here the forest floor was no deadening carpet of pine needles but a vivid maze of heather, blaeberry, juniper and birch scrub. Lichens and mosses draped from the trees. Birds twittered out of sight. Places such as this gave me hope, and it felt right that this was the place where I explained to my wife why I wanted to leave her for a month and go in search of some ultimate ideal of solitude, of wildness. This sanctuary gave my idea all the context it needed.

'Promise me something,' Hannah said as we got going again. 'I know you want to be disconnected, but I don't want you to be totally out of contact for a month.'

I'd considered this. Much as I sometimes fantasised about the monk-like isolation of my dad aboard *Yorrel*, I doubted I could withstand a month of being totally cut off from my loved ones with no contact at all. Although Hannah might have reluctantly agreed if I'd said I needed to do so, she would hate it, worry constantly about me – and not without good reason. Much could go wrong, and catastrophically so, on a winter

CWT. My mum would flat-out refuse. In fact, the very idea could be a major blow to her mental health. She had suffered from bouts of depression since Dad died, and I wanted to make this as easy for her as possible – it was already going to be hard enough.

Besides, a total disconnection would be jarringly artificial, even in the vast signal blackspots of the Scottish Highlands. This was always going to be artificial to some degree, of course. That couldn't be avoided. In a way it was almost the point. Hiking the Cape Wrath Trail in winter was going to be tough in itself, though, with countless potential dangers, and I wasn't going to risk my life for this project.

'I'll keep using my phone for calls and texts,' I said, 'and I've been in touch with a company that makes satellite trackers. The magazine's been negotiating with them, actually. They're going to sponsor whatever I write about the trip in *The Great Outdoors*, and I'll take one of their satellite communicators along with me. That means I'll be able to check in every day even if there's no phone signal.'

Her shoulders relaxed. 'That sounds better.' She turned and looked back to me with a sarcastic expression, but playful rather than unkind. 'You're really going to leave me to deal with all the crap at home by myself for a month, aren't you?'

Multiple family deaths, my mum's depression, her grandma's terminal illness, the ongoing process of trying to sell her grandad's house in Sheffield, and the birth of our niece Ada had all led to the last year or so feeling crammed with big stuff to think about and manage. I did feel a little guilty at checking out for a while, but Hannah had her mum on hand to help, and – honestly – I needed this. It was not going to be a holiday, but a trial by ice, perhaps, to find out who I was now. To find out what was wrong and how I could fix it.

We walked back through the woods in companionable silence, engaged in nature's marvels and the rare, perfect pleasure of time just for us, no work or family demands intruding. More squirrels capered in the swaying pine boughs above. Hannah squeezed my hand as we watched them. She had always loved red squirrels, because their fur is the same colour as her hair – autumnal bracken, sunlight on copper. It had been my favourite colour long before I'd met her, and to me it had always whispered of time spent alone in a forest glade, silent and attuned, letting myself dissolve. There's love in that too.

Perhaps what I was truly seeking was not some idealised solitude, but another kind of love that could only be felt by a deep and uncompromising immersion in the natural world. As I looked at Hannah, something I couldn't do without a special kind of aching wonder, I knew that she already understood this about me – she had always known what I needed to feel whole. Perhaps this quest was the one I'd known all my life, every time I felt the urge to vanish into the mountains for another taste of that greater journey. There were other forces acting on me, I realised then – older, more vital, more insistent – than the jittery urge to check my phone.

Much later, lying in bed and listening to the rain patter on the windows, I felt a sense of hope building in me, stronger than I'd felt in a long time.

PART 2

Wildtrack

Chapter 3

Day 1: 6 February 2019, Ardnamurchan Point, Scotland

'Did you lose a bet or something?'

On the long trudge out from the ferry at Kilchoan to the lighthouse at Ardnamurchan Point, where I would officially begin my walk, a local stopped to ask me if I wanted a lift. I'd added a warm layer beneath my waterproof jacket and was just pulling my gloves back on when the car pulled over and the driver wound down his window. I could see him eyeing up the rucksack towering over my head and shoulders. His gaze lingered on the massive blue snowshoes strapped to the sides of my pack. After I'd thanked him and turned down his offer, he'd asked where I was headed – 'The North Pole?' – and shook his head in amazement when I said I was on my way to Cape Wrath. He wished me luck with an expression that said he expected to read about my demise on a Mountain Rescue blog in the near future, and then wound his window back up and sped away into the rain.

This walk was already feeling very different to how I'd pictured it.

In the days before my journey up to Scotland, and on the journey itself, I'd stressed myself silly over worries beyond my control. What if my resupply parcels failed to get to their destinations? Many of the shops CWT hikers used to replenish their supplies were shut over the winter, so I'd sent pre-packaged supply boxes to various hostels and hotels along the way. I hadn't been able to confirm that all of them had arrived. Worse, I'd made a stupid error. Some of the supply boxes contained gas cartridges for my stove. In the frenzy of preparations, it hadn't occurred to me to check whether or not this was allowed. A tweet from a follower on the eve of my departure – 'Maybe we'll hear about an explosion at the Royal Mail depot on the news!' – had sent my anxiety into overdrive, and I'd fallen into the familiar cycle of berating myself for my mistakes and believing that if I couldn't be perfect then I might as well not even try.

Somehow, through the spiral of negative thinking and my mind flitting from one catastrophic scenario to the next, obsessing on the prospect of failure after building this trip up for so long in my head, I'd made it to the peninsula of Ardnamurchan. The walk was happening. It was real.

Although Fort William is the usual starting point for the Cape Wrath Trail, I had decided to extend my walk by starting at Ardnamurchan Point instead and joining the main route at Glenfinnan. At that moment, freezing cold and soaked through to my base layer, I questioned whether I'd been of sound mind to add several days of hard hiking to what would already be the hardest thing I'd ever done. From Glenfinnan, the Cape Wrath Trail would head north through the wildest and most remote mountain country until the land ran out beneath my feet.

Ardnamurchan Point is commonly cited as the westernmost point of the British mainland, although that isn't true – Corrachadh Mòr, a headland about a kilometre to the south, juts a few metres more into the sea. Nevertheless, I'd chosen Ardnamurchan Point as the start of my walk. Just like Cape Wrath, it was home to a lighthouse, and the symmetry of this idea appealed to me, walking from lighthouse to lighthouse between the westernmost (well, close enough) and northwesternmost points of the British mainland.

The lighthouse jutted like an obscene gesture on the horizon. Bands of rain scurried in front of it. It protruded from a foreground of rock the colour of weathered lead, dappled with bone-white blotches of lichen and a few tufts of grass that fringed pools of rainwater. Even the puddles had waves on them. The wind battered me, slammed against me. Out at sea, great roaring waves swept in from an indistinct horizon to pound at the shoreline while a few intrepid gulls fought the gusts, first dipping low then wheeling high before uttering calls that pierced through the background noise of water and storm.

I clambered back over the rocks to the road. My huge pack felt cumbersome, and the straps were already digging in to my shoulders. I couldn't remember the last time I'd carried a pack this heavy, weighed down with winter kit, backpacking essentials and food for over a week.

Rust-streaked outbuildings clustered around the lighthouse. There was an air of shabbiness and abandonment about this place, as if the landscape couldn't wait to reclaim it. People had not lived here for years; the light itself was now fully automated, although a café and visitors' centre served tourists between April and October. I peered through one of the windows into the café after wiping the raindrops away with a soggy glove. Inside, nothing but darkness.

After taking shelter around the side of the building, I dropped my pack again and pulled out the blocky orange satellite communicator I had on loan for the trip. Time to send my first check-in message.

The device took a few seconds to boot up. With its QWERTY keyboard, monochrome display and plastic antenna sticking out of the top, it looked a bit like an old-school BlackBerry. Similar devices, popular with backpackers, let you send pre-programmed messages to contacts, activate an emergency beacon, and (optionally) provide real-time tracking. Thanks to its built-in keyboard, this upgraded model could also be used as a two-way text messenger.

I activated the check-in function, which would – hopefully – send an automatic message to Hannah, my mum, my brother, and a few friends and colleagues who wanted to keep tabs on my progress. The progress indicator on the screen took forever to clear, and there was no positive confirmation that my message had actually sent. My tests prior to the trail hadn't inspired confidence. Some check-ins worked, while others failed silently, giving the operator no indication that the message hadn't gone through. The device triggered complex feelings in me. If I needed to press the SOS button, would it work? And what if two or more consecutive check-ins failed – at what point would my family decide that I needed to be rescued? Would its very presence change my behaviour or somehow tarnish the experience? Like my smartphone, would it remain as an ethereal presence in my mind even when switched off?

The satellite communicator went back into the top pocket of my rucksack. I had not activated the live tracking feature. I was willing to accept a lifeline, but I was not willing to be continuously tracked by the machine world I wanted to get away from. This line in the sand, I realised, was as arbitrary as the whole thing, but it felt important – why, otherwise, was I doing this at all?

At just after two o'clock in the afternoon I took my first step on the lighthouse-to-lighthouse walk that I hoped would lead me to Cape Wrath. At that moment, Cape Wrath felt incalculably distant – an objective so remote that it had become abstract, a symbol belonging to a future version of me not yet hammered into being.

***

When hiking in the Scottish Highlands, it can be tempting to romanticise the landscape as an unspoilt wilderness. This supports a narrative of the backpacker as an intrepid explorer experiencing life beyond civilisation's margins, but it's less than half of the whole truth, and ignores two crucial facts. First, people still live and work here despite a long and sad history of rural depopulation; and second, what looks like wilderness to the uneducated eye is anything but. Humans created this landscape. Humans destroyed the forests and killed much of the wildlife. Humans are responsible not only for conservation successes but also for nature-hostile forms of land use that suppress biodiversity – and even the economic potential of human communities. There's plenty of wildness in the West Highlands, but in most areas it's a landscape created by intensive grazing by sheep and deer, the slaughter of predators and the clearance of crofting populations. The result is a landscape with as few as two people per square kilometre in some large areas.[1] It can seem empty, and it can certainly feel bleak and wild, but twenty per cent of Scotland is covered by deer-stalking estates – including many of the areas traversed by the Cape Wrath Trail.

The wildness we see today is a result of centuries of failure: failure to

1 Macdonald, *Rebirding: Rewilding Britain and its Birds*, 128

make the land work for the populations who once lived here, and failure to protect the natural abundance we have now mostly lost. What's left is an impoverished landscape of drastically simplified ecosystems where fewer people are able to make a living from the land.

These were the negative thoughts that swirled around my head as I trudged through the rain, the wind at my back pushing me along the boggy path. When I looked up from my head-down slog, I saw a deer fence six feet high entangled with scraps of sodden bracken, dirty dishcloths in the dim light.

The weather began to improve, lifting my mood with it, as I descended towards the crofting township of Portuairk beside Sanna Bay. I saw a row of small white cottages set against a fractal landscape of rock and sand, breaking surf and bladderwrack. Stands of birch trees sprouted here and there above the high-tide mark. There was a red phone box by the side of the single-track road. This, clearly, was a working settlement – although much later I discovered that Portuairk had been established as late as 1843, settled by crofters evicted from elsewhere on the Ardnamurchan Estate.

The trail took me north out of Portuairk, then across a small but deep and fast-flowing river that I had no alternative but to ford. I considered taking off my boots and gaiters and crossing barefoot, but I was already feeling cold; the idea of a bone-numbing wade through that torrent in bare feet didn't appeal. Besides, I thought as I stood on the bank and tried to gauge the surging peat-brown water, it didn't look that deep. I took my first step away from the bank. My gaiter kept the water out for about two seconds before it poured into my boot and I felt a slow, cold wetness spread from ankle to toe. When I took a second step, the water came up almost to the knee, and I teetered there in the fast-moving stream, adjusting to the pressure on my legs and trying to identify the safest way across. My rucksack's massive weight on my back suddenly felt like a liability. I leant against my trekking poles into the current and took calculated strides into the centre, skirting a pool so deep I couldn't see the bottom. By the time I dragged myself out on the far bank I could feel the river water sloshing about in my boots.

The day was fading fast, and so was my motivation. Time to look for somewhere to camp.

***

Scotland has some of the most enlightened laws in the world when it comes to 'wild' camping. The right to set up a tent on unenclosed land for a night or two is enshrined in law, and this is one reason why Scotland is the best part of the UK for backpacking. In the Scottish Highlands, you can camp wherever you like provided that you are sensitive to the environment and leave no trace of your presence.

A sand dune firmed up with moss and marram grass rose above the white sands of Sanna Bay, providing a flat and well-drained spot just big enough for me to pitch my tent. An unhurried surf rolled in a few hundred yards away, and the high winds had blown away inland, taking the murk and rain and hopelessness with them, and patches of sky the palest blue now glimmered behind a veil of high-level cloud. I'd take it.

As always, the first night under canvas felt awkward. Unpacking all my gear seemed to take forever. There was the tent itself to pitch, a new model on test that I'd received only days before the trip and hadn't had the chance to try out beforehand. It went up in about twenty minutes – a surprisingly large green dome, its stormworthiness overkill for this benign spot but I hoped it would stand up to far harsher camps later in the trail. Then I had to inflate my sleeping mat, test its squidge with a hand, roll out my fluffy sleeping bag, find places to stow all the little knick-knacks that seem to breed in rucksack pockets. After an hour or so, I was sitting in the tent porch with a pan of water on the boil, my stove roaring gently. I'd changed into my warm sleeping clothes and the surf's lullaby was making me feel content and sleepy. Wild camping has a way of making anxieties and discomfort seem far away, and in that moment, watching the golden evening light play on the rippling grass of sand dunes and letting my mind drift out to sea, I knew that in attempting this journey I was doing the right thing.

***

Day 2: 7 February 2019

I woke at just after seven o'clock the next morning to find several small puddles on the groundsheet inside my tent. Condensation had been heavy overnight – always a risk in winter, with low temperatures and damp air – and my tent's magic breathable fabric had failed to wick away the condensation as advertised. As I shone my head torch beam over the inside of my tent, I could see droplets of moisture clinging to the fabric and trickling down the sides to pool on the sewn-in groundsheet. A drip landed on my forehead. With a start, I realised that the foot end of my sleeping bag had been pressed up against the tent wall and was now a sodden ball of porridge, the down saturated and clumped. No wonder my feet felt cold.

As I packed away my camp, despondency and self-criticism seized me. I should have got my gear for this trip sorted well in advance. I should have had time to properly test such a crucial item as my tent – should have made sure it was up to the job. I'd been so picky about the shelter I chose for this trip, making sure it was able to withstand fierce gales and snow-loading, but the breathable fabric had been a gamble that hadn't paid off. Either I was expecting too much from the technology or I'd received a faulty sample. How would it cope with tougher conditions in the mountains further north?

***

After a few hours, I found myself back at the village of Kilchoan where I'd come off the ferry from Mull the previous day. I'd drawn a cross-country route on the map, across the rim of the ancient volcanic caldera that had once formed the peninsula of Ardnamurchan but was now visible only from space or by scrutinising contour lines on a map sheet. After climbing away from Sanna Bay on the road and reaching the point where my route headed across the wild open landscape towards the rim of crags where lava once flowed, I found that I didn't have the motivation for it. Faced by more deer fences blocking my way, and huge stretches of blanket bog where the wind ruffled open water and made stands of rushes sway, I took the road instead, feeling like a failure. *It's a marathon, not a sprint,* I told myself. At least the weather had turned sunny, and in the warm February light the grasses, heather and bracken of the landscape glowed a vivid bronze.

Back at Kilchoan, I couldn't resist another visit to the village stores for some snacks, even though I had all the food I needed.

'We dinna get many hikers at this time of year,' said the small woman who worked the till. She wore an apron and a fixed, kind smile. 'Where are you headed?'

'Cape Wrath,' I said, and immediately felt like a fraud. At that moment, I didn't believe that I'd make it that far.

***

Day 3: 8 February 2019

I didn't get much sleep on my second night. The steady drip, drip of condensation from the soaked fabric of my tent woke me every hour with a rising, irrepressible anxiety. I mopped at the water I could see swelling at the seams, trying to catch it before it pooled on the tent floor, but it was hopeless – the condensation formed faster than I could mop it up. I'd even kept the tent door partially open to increase airflow, and left my damp clothes in the porch. Nothing worked. The tent was already soggy from the night before. An unstoppable chain reaction unfolded before my eyes. I gathered up my gear and tried to pile it as close to the centre of the groundsheet as possible, away from the growing puddles at the edges. By about two o'clock in the morning, steady rain, hard and getting harder, was lashing against my shelter along with a rising gale, thrumming at the guylines and pounding at the tent walls. Soon the condensation was flying in all directions – my own private indoor rainstorm. *I can't continue the trail with this tent,* was the thought that kept coming back again and again as I worried and overthought the problem. *Maybe I can't continue at all. Maybe I'm not tough enough for this.*

When my alarm went off at 7.30, I shifted in my sleeping bag and delayed the moment of switching on my head torch and seeing the extent of the damage. As I wriggled my bare toes, I realised that the inside of my sleeping bag now felt as damp as the outside had felt the previous night.

My head torch illuminated the glistening surfaces of dry bags, into which I'd packed my clothes, piled up next to my sleeping mat to try and keep them away from the puddles at the edges of the groundsheet. The groundsheet itself sloshed with water. I could see a puddle the size of Windermere down at the foot end. As I sat up, the lake shifted and threatened to pour back in my direction to engulf my camera bag and phone, which I'd propped up adjacent to my head and shoulders.

As a child in the Scouts my Bible had been *The Backpacker's Handbook* by Chris Townsend – an outdoor writer who, many years later, had become a colleague. One idea from this book had stuck in my mind: keep your sleeping bag dry, because your life could depend on it. I could feel the dampness through my sleeping clothes. The yellow outer fabric of my sleeping bag shone wetly in the torchlight. This was not a good situation.

As I sat there and wondered what to do, a solution came to me at once. I tried to unthink it just as quickly, come up with something better, but no rational alternative came to mind. This was how it was going to happen.

I took my iPhone and thumbed the airplane mode icon, then waited for a moment to see if any signal had miraculously appeared in this dank hollow on the edge of a forestry plantation, which of course it hadn't. I could wander up the hill looking for signal, but time was going to be critical, so, hating myself a little, I fished the orange satellite communicator out of the top pocket of my pack and switched it on. I entered text messaging mode and laboriously typed out a message on its cramped keys:

TO: Hannah. Please send bivvy bag in orange sac, tent (in dark brown sac) and bathtub groundsheet (small grn sac) to James asap. Must arrive by Monday.

Then I hit the send button and hoped for the best. As I watched the screen, angling the antenna towards the sky and waiting for the sending icon to disappear, I realised that my message might worry Hannah without context. I composed a second text, explaining the problem and telling her there was nothing to worry about.

As I packed up my sodden gear and stuffed it into my sodden rucksack, I couldn't shake a sense of failure – that in reaching out for help over my electronic lifeline I had already compromised the spirit of what I was trying to do. The very presence of a satellite communicator had changed my behaviour. I had not even tried to come up with a solution on my own because I'd known there was an easier option. I didn't want to risk my life for no reason, but where did I draw the line? Start chipping away at the shaky foundations of self-sufficiency and isolation underpinning what is, let's face it, an artificial challenge, and you might as well go on a bus trip to Cape Wrath instead.

Before I started walking again, I took a moment to look around. The sky, magnificently impressive, lowered over me in ragged layers overlapping each other as they swirled over the brows of the hills. A group of hinds watched me with a stag from the boggy hillside beneath Ben Hiant, where a few snow patches persisted against the wind and rain. I saw that the night's weather had given fresh energy to the small burn that flared and gurgled beside my campsite. This was a beautiful place, but my mind was too stuffed with anxieties to appreciate it.

***

Day 4: 9 February 2019

The wind blew me off my feet on the way down to Acharacle. Savage gusts howled over the open land. The stands of trees that had somehow found a foothold despite the sheep and the deer crouched down against the onslaught, braced and shivering.

I blundered over the cushions of heather and bleached bracken straw, feeling cumbersome and a little out of control with my monstrous pack swaying to and fro on my back like a counterweight, catching the wind's edge and sapping my energy. Stinging rain followed soon enough. I started to worry about my camera in its shoulder bag. Although the camera was theoretically weather resistant, and I'd stuffed it inside a dry bag for another layer of defence, I hadn't been able to resist taking it out for a shot of the wave-strafed sea, and now the camera was running with water and the lens fogged. Backpacking could be hard on photographic gear and I couldn't afford a camera failure this early in the trip.

When I came to the road I made the easy choice and diverted along my foul-weather alternative. The off-path route I'd planned over the hills seemed ludicrous to me now, the product of a more optimistic, more comfortable state of mind back at home, when the hardships of the trail were abstract and unknowable.

***

'The tent's leaking a bit, that's all. No huge drama.'

I'd finally found a bar or two of signal along the coast road and, fumbling with numbed fingers, dialled Hannah to let her know what was going on.

'I was worried when the message came through,' she said. 'Just one message telling me to send your spare tent ASAP with no explanation. What happened?'

'Did you not get my second message explaining it all?'

'No. Just the first, then silence. I've sent you about five texts.'

As she spoke, my phone vibrated and a handful of her messages appeared. 'Are you ok?xxx' one of them said, then the next: 'Been to the post office posted your tent. Hope you're ok.xxx'

'My second message from the communicator must have failed,' I said. 'Bloody thing.'

I talked her through the events of the last couple of nights on the trail.

'Condensation puddles,' she said once I'd finished. 'I thought your tent had collapsed or something. I've spent hours imagining the worst.'

'That's why I tried to send the second message,' I said, feeling a little foolish. Had I overreacted after all?

'At least the first message came through,' she said, 'even if it did wake me up with a shock. I've been to the post office, anyway. James should receive the parcel tomorrow. He's bringing a supply box up to you at Glenfinnan, isn't he?' Her tone sounded a little exasperated. 'I've been tracking your resupply parcels online,' she added. 'They've all arrived safely.'

My resupply parcels were critical. If I arrived at the Kintail Lodge Hotel on the other side of Knoydart and found my first supply box missing, I could be forced to take an entire day off from the trail, hitching or taking the bus miles down the road to find an open shop. I was still worrying about the gas canisters in some of the boxes too, and my stupid mistake in posting them. What if there had been an error with the tracking and one of the boxes had been destroyed or diverted instead? What if a box had been left outside in the rain and forgotten about? I forced myself to be optimistic.

'I'm sure,' she said in response to my unasked question. 'Don't worry. You're doing so well.'

***

By the time I got to the tiny coastal village of Salen late in the afternoon, I knew that camping was out of the question that night. There comes a time on every long-distance walk when you've gone past the point where you should have stopped for the night – when it's too dark, your gear is too soaked and the idea of finding somewhere decent to camp in a waterlogged landscape is about as realistic as hiking to the moon. I hit that point a couple of kilometres before reaching Salen, which looked like nothing more than a watery smudge of reflected electric light as I staggered downhill through the only street to the shoreline. Breakers crashed in off the loch. I couldn't see them in the darkness, but I could hear them – an echoing, rolling roar competing with the wind. A sign flapped in the beam of my head torch: 'SALEN HOUSE B&B'. This would do.

I pushed open the door and stood in the porch dripping all over the floor. After only a moment, the inner door opened and a small figure stood there silhouetted against the light streaming out from inside. Once my eyes adjusted, I saw a middle-aged lady with an expression of be-mused surprise spreading over her face. She was squinting at me, and I realised that my head torch was still on. I turned it off.

'Do you have a room for the night?'

She hesitated before answering. 'Certainly not a night for camping. We have just the double room at the moment. It'll be fifty-five pounds.'

***

That night, I slept fitfully despite the room's comfort. I had a double bed with soft white sheets to luxuriate in, all to myself. Even though I'd only been on the trail for a few days, already the bed felt too comfortable, too large, too empty, its expanse serving to remind me that I usually shared a double bed with my wife, and she was hundreds of miles away.

Art prints on the wall, vague blurs in the darkness, depicted Scottish coastal scenes. The fusty aroma of drying hill clothes filled my nostrils, a curiously nostalgic fug that always took me back to climbing trips as a teenager and youth hostels and cheaper beer. In the absence of a drying room, the single radiator in my B&B room was doing its best; I'd draped it with clothes and arranged more on chairs positioned around it. It was a wonder any heat managed to escape through the damp layers of fabric at all. My saturated boots, when I'd pulled them off, had steamed.

Precisely one year before, I'd been trying to sleep in the visitors' room on Ward 7a, with starlings chattering outside the window.

I'd known, of course, that the anniversary was approaching, and that it would come as an invader of my solitude while I was on the trail – but I didn't know how it would come. As a marauder, or as a gentler presence? Would I feel closer to my father on the anniversary of his death, or further away? I lay there in the dark, listening to the gale's fading energy outside. A year ago I hadn't slept holding Hannah close to me either, although I think I'd reached out to touch her hand a few times as she slouched in the other chair, a coffee table and stack of well-thumbed magazines between us. This time there was no solace of contact.

Everything about the long walk ahead felt wrong. I'd ended up soaked and storm-battered in a B&B after only a few days, having walked only thirty-one miles. Cape Wrath felt further away than ever. Did I really think I could cope with the harder and higher terrain to the north at this time of year on a long-distance trail? I'd already had one gear failure. My pack was far too heavy, slowing me down. A sense had been building since I walked away from the lighthouse at Ardnamurchan Point that I could not do this.

I forced myself to accept that the negativity would pass, but the moment of loneliness wasn't so easily banished. The smartphone on my bedside table, a dormant slab, whispered to me. Although I'd rigged it to be incapable of accessing the internet, there were ways around that if my willpower crumbled. There would be Wi-Fi here. Bright hits of dopamine delivered by apps – digital anaesthesia, a fuzzy smoothing-over of reality as I sank back into no-time – were only a few taps away.

I resisted the temptation, but I didn't feel virtuous for doing so. It felt meaningless and harsh. The raw feelings sloshed around in my skull and there was nothing to do but confront them.

Chapter 4

Day 5: 10 February 2019

For much of that afternoon, my companion on the trail had been a golden eagle. As I'd crept over a landscape of water and tussocky grass and exposed, eroding peat, the eagle had soared high overhead – a broad-fingered silhouette tracing bright lines on the grey sky. At times it drew close enough that I could see the hook of its beak as it angled its head down towards me, as if calculating the likelihood of my becoming carrion in the near future. More often it wheeled high above, but I was constantly aware of my watcher as I made my way to Corryhully bothy and the end of the first section of my Cape Wrath Trail. It had been a long, hard day with more road walking than I'd planned.

The eagle left me just before I arrived at Corryhully bothy. It flickered over the river like a ghost, disturbing two young stags who were rooting about in last year's faded bracken on the far bank, and then it was gone, flying fast in a straight line back west towards Loch Beoraid. It gave a little 'yip' just as it vanished out of sight. My world felt brightened. The eagle knew what lay on the other side of the mountain wall to the north; it could no doubt see into Knoydart from its high vantage point. I could only imagine and worry about the hardships ahead. Perhaps I should try to be more like the eagle.

Corryhully, which I'd last visited late the previous year during my Knoydart recce trip, would be my home for the next two nights. The long, squat shape of the shelter protruded as a singularity of human meaning in a landscape of natural textures and shapes (natural except for the access track and jarring new hydro dams, that is). Bothies are chameleons. Sometimes they camouflage themselves perfectly; at other times they stick out for miles around, beacons of warmth and shelter. Corryhully had always been a beacon to me.

I pushed open the door and stepped into the dark, barn-like interior. My eyes took a few moments to adjust, but I began to make out splashes of form in the darkness, painted by a dull glow from small, square windows: a rough bench, a table with an old kettle and some bottles on it, and a knackered old chair. The right-hand end of the single long room, farthest away from the fireplace, was always darkest, coldest and dampest. I turned away from the deeper shadows there and dumped my gear on the bench as close to the fireplace as possible.

It was not much warmer inside than out, and I could hear rain drumming on the corrugated iron roof. After dumping my pack, I took the satellite device out of its pocket and stepped back outside to send my check-in for the day, which would tell friends and family that I'd arrived safely at Corryhully. I waited for a few minutes, pointed the antenna at the snow-filled clouds above, and pressed the button. Would it work this time? I had no real way of knowing. Although I'd been cursing the device's unreliability, at that moment I found that I appreciated its lack of feedback, its refusal to connect me back to the glowing datasphere I was trying to hide from for a while.

***

They say that the outdoors is a balm for anxiety, but I've never found that to be entirely true. My more ambitious trips sometimes give me even more to worry about while I'm hiking. Adventurous worries replace mundane ones. The beautiful simplicity of life on foot can be elusive.

That evening, as I sat swaddled in down jacket and sleeping bag listening to the ping of rain on the roof and the spit and crackle of fire in the fireplace, I wrote a list in my journal of all the things I was worrying about. I wrote that I was still concerned about my resupply parcels, even though Hannah had checked the tracking and confirmed they were all delivered safely. I dwelt on my restlessness at having to stay put and wait a whole day at Corryhully for James to receive my tent and bring it to me. Then I started worrying about conditions further north, if this was all a stupid idea and I was not capable of doing what I'd set out to do. This wasn't just a personal challenge; I'd been commissioned to write a series of articles for the magazine. 'Much depends on what I manage to achieve,' I wrote. 'While failure could be a successful outcome (failures can make the best stories), if I'm going to fail it has to be an interesting failure. It's mad that I find myself worrying about exactly how I'm going to fail. It's like being in the trenches at the Somme and worrying more about where the bullet will hit me than if I'm going to be hit at all. Have I already convinced myself that failure is inevitable? Cape Wrath feels a hell of a long way away.'

Writing all this down hardly made me feel better, but at least it quantified the seething doubts in my head. After a while I put down my pen, closed my notebook, crept out of my sleeping bag into the cold, and poured myself a large dram from one of the bottles left behind by a previous visitor. Whisky bottles left behind in bothies are usually empty and have candle stubs crammed down their necks, but I'd found bottles of Aberlour, Ardmore, Nevis Dew and Navy Rum all with several drams left; the Nevis Dew was almost half full.

Then the door creaked open and more head torches lit up the inside of the bothy. Two figures, jackets sleek with rainwater, stepped inside. The door slammed behind them.

'Hey! There's someone here already!'

'An' there's a fire! Fucking brilliant, mate. Get in.'

***

My new friends, Mike and Louis, settled in and sprawled their kit all over the rest of the bothy. Mike, I soon learnt, was a junior doctor; Louis had just finished a master's in physiotherapy. Both were in their mid-twenties and experienced hillwalkers, but neither had visited a bothy before. I think they were a little surprised to find someone else. My roaring fire soon drew them into conversation and before long we were all perched on chairs or logs in the circle of its comforting glow, clasping whisky glasses and swapping stories of the hills.

'We're heading for Inverie,' Mike told me. 'Through Knoydart, across to Glen Pean bothy. Do you think the weather will hold?'

I listened for a moment. The rain on the roof had stopped, and a heavy silence penetrated the bothy's interior, broken only by the occasional hiss and pop from the fire. 'Let's take a look outside.'

I lurched to my feet. The whisky had done its work. The air felt freezing only a pace or two away from the fire, and I could feel the concrete floor stealing the warmth from my feet even through my fluffy socks and plastic slippers. I opened the door. After a few moments my eyes adjusted to the deeper darkness outside and I beheld a sky crammed full of twinkling stars, so many more than I was used to seeing back down south. There was a persistent glow too, coming from the cirque of mountains above me and crowding around the glen – not the moon, but the softer glow of starlight on fresh snow. A glow that spoke to a younger version of me, the ambitious climber who had once lived for the bite of ice axes and crampons in dark gullies under the full moon. That part of me stirred once again, responding to the nameless emotion that rained down on me from the stars above. Or maybe it was the glow of ten-year-old Aberlour in an empty stomach. Thinking back to my days as a climbing-obsessed barman in Glen Coe, I recalled that it could be hard to tell the difference.

The rain that had depressed my spirits had been dumping as snow on the high tops. Winter was back, the skies were clear, and I could feel the frost biting.

An hour later, after we'd polished off a respectable proportion of the whisky and had just chucked one of the bigger logs on the fire, we heard the bothy door creak open once again.

In staggered a young man with a tiny rucksack and a thousand-yard stare. My immediate thought, influenced no doubt by the whisky, was that he looked like a scarecrow who had been built from mismatched items of cutting-edge ultralight outdoor gear. Tall, lanky, with unkempt hair and intense eyes, the newcomer lurched and swayed on the threshold for a moment before dragging his phone out from his pocket and thumbing the touchscreen. Its glow illuminated a face etched with fatigue. He looked strikingly young.

'This is Corryhully, right?' he said, looking up from the screen. 'Actually maybe I'll head to the next bothy. I'm behind on my mileage target.'

I looked at my watch. It was ten o'clock at night.

'Screw that,' Mike or Louis said from behind me. 'It's miles. Get a dram inside you. And shut the door, aye?'

'Right, sorry.' He shut the door and pulled off his pack, then stood there for a moment as if he didn't know what to do. 'Maybe I'll just stop for a rest and some Super Noodles.'

After rummaging in his pack, the newcomer set up a gas stove on one of the wooden sleeping platforms and positioned a tall titanium mug full of water on top of it. The stove roared, but before the water was boiled he had ripped open a pack of Super Noodles and broken the contents into the steaming mug.

He poked at it with a long-handled spoon as I stood a few paces away, whisky in hand. 'What's your name?' I said. 'I'm Alex, and the others are Mike and Louis.' The others waved from their seats, which were as close to the fire as they could get them.

The young man with the floppy blond hair said, 'My name's Skye. I'm just starting the Cape Wrath Trail leg of my LEJOG.'

'Bloody hell.'

Skye puffed up visibly at my reaction. LEJOG stood for Land's End to John o'Groats – an end-to-end hike of the British mainland. Doing it via the Cape Wrath Trail, in winter, was LEJOG on hard mode.

He poked at his Super Noodles again. The top-heavy mug fell over, spilling boiling liquid all over his sleeping area. 'Shit,' he said, grabbing at the mug and burning his fingers in the process. He managed to scoop most of the noodles back into his mug.

Mike and Louis had sauntered over, muffled in fleeces and woolly hats. Skye looked at the others before his gaze darted to me, perhaps sensing that I was the oldest.

'So I guess you guys are pretty experienced at all this?' Skye said, his casual tone not quite hiding what I interpreted as an underlying nervousness, or maybe a need to prove his own mountain cred. I tried to pin his accent down. It was plummy, perhaps private school.

'Not really,' I said, then realised that my reflexive self-effacing reply wasn't strictly true any more. 'I've been hillwalking and mountaineering for about sixteen years.'

Skye's eyes visibly widened. 'Gosh.'

'We've been doing this for a few years too,' Louis said. 'This is our first real backpacking trip together, though.'

Mike peered at Skye for a moment before asking the question we were all thinking. 'So how old *are* you?'

His reply came out in a rush. 'Sixteen, actually. I finished my GCSEs last year. I'm hiking bits of this trail in between studying for my A levels, but I've got big plans – I want to hike the HRP, maybe the PCT. I won't have much time for studying.' He stopped and looked at me. 'You haven't seen my parents, have you? They're following me, sort of. I pretty much ran away to go hiking.'

Mike whistled. 'You ran away from home to hike across Britain? At sixteen? Hardcore, man. Fair play to you.'

'Well, only sort of,' Skye said uncertainly. When he spoke again, his tone was surprisingly confident, almost fierce. 'Mum and Dad know where I am, because I have to carry a bloody satellite tracker. They keep trying to meet up. It's playing hell with my mileage targets.'

It was a strange feeling to be the oldest person in the bothy for a change rather than the youngest. Skye's awkward enthusiastic bluster, his youth, his vulnerability that he was so earnestly trying to hide, added up to someone whose life would be changed beyond recognition by the Cape Wrath Trail.

'What are your plans for the next section of the trail?' I probed.

In between scooping lukewarm noodles into his mouth, Skye asked me rapid-fire questions about the trail. I filled him in on river crossings (especially the missing Carnach bridge I'd been worrying about for so long), likely winter conditions, route variants and navigational challenges. Although his daily mileage targets were ambitious, he seemed to have his head screwed on the right way. I soon adjusted the level of my advice. It was clear that he was more experienced and better prepared than I'd initially supposed. He explained that he hoped to stay in bothies as much as possible because his ultralight US-made tent was proving hopeless with condensation. I told him about my own tent woes, and that I had to wait another day for my brother to bring a replacement tent over from Inverness.

'You are both gear nerds of the highest order,' Louis said with a laugh after slurping the last of his whisky. 'Is this what bothies are all about, then? Male bonding over shit tents and getting pished?'

We returned to the fireside, and budged up to make room for Skye. I picked up the bottle of Nevis Dew and shook it, swilling the malt around in the bottom, looking at the others. Mike and Louis both nodded; Skye looked uncertain.

'I've never had whisky before,' he said, and then, 'I guess I won't get to the next bothy tonight after all. I'll get my mug.'

By the look in his eyes after gulping it down, he needed that.

'How are you funding this epic hike, then?' Louis said after a few minutes of companionable silence.

'I make custom ultralight gear for hikers,' Skye said, 'and also buy and sell coins on eBay, that kind of stuff. It's mostly self-funded.'

'Fair play,' Mike said again. 'Skye, you are a legend.'

I poured everyone another dram, and Louis pitched another log on to the fire. My worries could not have been further from my mind.

***

Day 6: 11 February 2019

As Mike, Louis and I hiked uphill, boots crunching through concentric shims of ice that had been puddles the previous day, I kept stealing upward glances at our objective. The pyramidal summit of Sgùrr nan Coireachan gleamed a radiant white against the blue. The new snow line looked pristine maybe 500 metres above us.

Louis, a few paces ahead of me, turned to look back and asked me about likely conditions. It was a good excuse for a halt. We all paused for a moment, breathing hard from the steep uphill climb that was already warming me up despite the freezing air. I wondered if the others felt as hungover as I did. Their expressions told me they wished they weren't slogging uphill at half past eight in the morning. I'd been surprised when Mike and Louis said they wanted to join me on my climb of the two mountains above the bothy; for me it was a day walk, killing time until I could meet up with James, while for them it was set to be an alternative route to Glen Pean to take advantage of the snow and a rare window of fine weather.

Only one snag: Mike and Louis didn't have ice axes or crampons, because they hadn't expected them to be necessary. Their plan was to turn back if our ascent took them on to terrain where winter gear might be required. I'd examined their proposed route, dropping down to Glen Pean from the first summit, and it looked reasonable – but there were question marks about conditions. The presence of old, hard-frozen snow could make this route dangerous without winter gear.

'It's hard to say,' I replied, squinting upwards again. 'There might have been no more than a few inches of fresh snow, and it won't be consolidated.'

By the time we reached the snow line, and an abrupt steepening of the mountain ridge to a knuckled spine where outcrops broke through the white, the sun had come out and the others had warmed up so much that they'd stripped down to T-shirts. Sun, snow and blue skies blended into an intense mountain glare. I put on my sunglasses. Beneath us, mist curled in the valleys. I could see the greenish tinge of frost in meadows where the sun had not yet stripped it away. Sandwiched between the shadowed forests below and the snow above, hillsides burned a steady russet-gold in the sunshine, the colour of old bracken and deer grass.

The others were racing ahead of me and had soon vanished out of sight behind one of the many knolls on the ridge. I immediately felt better. It had been good to hike with company, but I've always been happiest in the mountains when alone.

I turned all my attention to the mountaineering problem immediately in front of me. The ridge, which had looked dramatic even from below, steepened to a high-angle ramp of hard, consolidated snow, blown clean of the recent fresh stuff by strong winds. We'd been wading through the odd snowdrift below, but I now realised that I wouldn't be able to safely tackle this slope without winter gear. A fall on a slope like that could kill me. I dropped my rucksack and dug out my crampons – lightweight frameworks of aluminium spikes, folded up in their special bag to prevent them from stabbing my clothes and other gear – and unstrapped my ice axe from the outside of my pack. After I'd fitted the crampons to my boots and held my axe in my right hand I felt better equipped.

For the first part of the slope, which gradually got steeper until it hit an angle of about thirty degrees (steeper than it sounds when you're climbing hard snow), I followed the footprints of Mike and Louis. They'd tackled the slope head-on, kicking steps with their boots; occasionally I saw the marks of fingers where one had steadied himself with a gloved hand. The line of steps wove from rock outcrop to rock outcrop for about ten metres before abruptly veering off left towards easier ground. Sensibly, they had decided not to tackle this slope after all without the necessary gear. I decided to catch up with them to find out what they planned to do next, and followed their line of steps traversing across the slope. Mike and Louis had dropped down from the face and had stopped for a snack at a level patch of snow nearby. They waved as I approached.

'Aye, you were right about conditions,' Mike said ruefully. 'Too sketchy without spikes up there, like.'

Louis squinted up into the sun as if trying to seek out an alternative line, but we all knew that this was as far as they could go without winter gear.

'What will you do now?' I asked them.

'We'll go back to the bothy, then take our original low-level route into Knoydart,' Louis said. 'Plenty of time yet. It's been nice to get up high and see the snow, anyway. Does the spirit good.'

'You're a jammy git heading up there on a day as good as today,' Mike added. 'I've rarely seen it so good. Don't take it for granted, aye?'

We shook hands and said our goodbyes.

***

As I climbed higher and a veil of cloud blew over the mountain, transforming it from benign dreamscape to a swirling place of cold winds and abstract forms, Mike's parting words echoed in my head, loose ends looking for connections.

Scottish mountains in winter are creatures of transcendence and wonder. They are in a state of constant flux. Snow falls, is driven and drifted by the wind, baked by the sun and hardened by the stars. As the weather changes, ever sculpting a living work of art, the aspirant mountaineer is left to wait for the optimum moment to attempt the climb – or to wait for another day. Snow and storm conspire to build the latent threat of avalanches. More often than not the snow is too soft, too deep or too wet; high winds or persistent low cloud can make the very idea of climbing ludicrous. Snatching an audience with the sublime can feel like a chance in a million. Sometimes bad forecast after bad forecast can turn the love sour and make us forget how revelatory it can be at its best.

But a mountain in winter is more like a delicate bird than a landscape, and as W.H. Murray once wrote in his classic book *Mountaineering in Scotland,* the wings do not grow of their own accord.

There are moments that flare through a life, illuminating everything that came before and everything that will come after. Breaking out into the pristine snowy bowl of Coire nan Lochan on a morning of such silence that I could hear my own heart, the sky blushing pink over the shoulder of Gearr Aonach, stars burning steady out of the cold depths. After heavy snowfall in May, contemplating the alpenglow-lit north face of Aonach Beag – a primal place belonging to atoms and frost and the slow turn of the heavens. Waking at midnight beneath a tarp pitched on the ridge of the Grey Corries to find the aurora dancing over the depths of Glen Spean, greens and purples flickering off the snow all around me, ten minutes of contemplation decompressing into a lifetime of rapture.

These experiences are precious because they are rare, and they are becoming rarer.

Living in Glen Coe a decade before, I'd come close to taking the splendour of Scotland's mountains in winter for granted. I'd been at hand for some of the best winter seasons in living memory. The mountains had been wreathed in snow for months on end, and I'd drunk my fill, treading the starry ways with ice axes and crampons. Perhaps I'd thought it would always be like that. But since then winters had grown leaner and meaner, granting less of the magic, bringing instead rain, gales and the bleak brown of bare hills. The world was heating up, the beauty fading more quickly than I could ever have feared. And I'd changed too, of course. The death of a parent had cast strange shadows within my soul.

Did I believe that I'd find what I was looking for on this winter Cape Wrath Trail? Perhaps it was an act of hope, an act of defiance. Of resistance.

As I neared the summit of Sgùrr nan Coireachan, hidden in the cloud one moment and revealed the next, I looked down and beheld the fractal whorls of sastrugi in the snow at my feet carved by the wind. Fine powder blasted across the ridge, binding and blinding me for a moment; when I looked up, the patterns in the snow had changed again, their previous formations gone forever. A time might come, I realised then, when a person could no longer stand near a Scottish summit and marvel at the fleeting beauty of sastrugi in a wind that decorated every stone with feathers of rime ice. A point when shifting baselines would erase this wonder along with all the others already lost in time. *Don't take it for granted.* For a moment I was overcome by gratitude.

When I reached the summit trig point, a concrete pillar coated with ice, the clouds lifted suddenly and I could see twenty or thirty miles north into Knoydart, towards the crux of my journey I'd worried about for so long. My eyes darted from summit to summit, seeking known landmarks. Crinkled mountains stretched ahead in all directions, clad in thick snow, rising above brown glens. There was Sgùrr na Cìche towering above its neighbouring peaks; there, along the ridge to its right, my pass of Bealach Coire nan Gall, which I'd crossed in December to check out alternative routes to avoid the missing bridge. It looked snowy for at least 200 metres below the col, and I was looking at its south side – there would be far more snow hidden from view on its steep north face. I filed that information away for future pondering and took a record shot with my camera to analyse later.

The landscape of the Cape Wrath Trail stretched out ahead of me for a wondrous minute: rugged, remote, untouchable, just as it should be. Then the curtain of cloud closed over me once again and I was back with my own thoughts in the white room. Frost, I realised, clogged my beard, and when I lifted my water bottle for a drink I found it plugged with ice. A fierce happiness coursed through my veins as I stamped in the snow and rubbed my gloved hands together to keep warm. In that moment, nothing but the experience mattered.

PART 3

Aurimmersion

Chapter 5

Day 7: 12 February 2019

The rain came down in torrents as I waited at the Glenfinnan visitor centre for James to arrive. The air had felt mild on the short walk back down the glen from the bothy to the road. Although cloud now hid the mountains from view, I had no doubt that most of yesterday's fresh snow was in the river by now.

The visitor centre wasn't open when I arrived just before nine o'clock. Feeling cold and starting to shiver after only a few minutes of standing still, I loitered under the covered area where, in the summer, tourists and the occasional bewildered CWT hiker could be seen clutching ice creams and coffees. Each time I heard a vehicle approaching along the road I looked up, hoping to see James's car slowing to a halt, but each time I was disappointed. A few hundred metres away across the road, the monument to the failed Jacobite rebellion broke the skyline – a stark monolith at the V between hills layered in mist.

As soon as the visitor centre opened, I shuffled inside and ordered something hot to eat and drink from the little café. Through the rain-spattered window I saw James walk past, hands in pockets and hunched against the weather; a tall, thin figure wrapped up in an old waterproof jacket. He gave a small wave and a rueful smile as he strode in front of the window.

'How's it going?' James said. 'Sorry I'm so late. Traffic was insane.'

'You haven't missed much. Did you bring my tent up with you? And the supply box?'

'Aye, they're in the car.' His accent always surprised me whenever we met up after a while apart. Although English, like me, he'd lived in Scotland for many years and the accent had rubbed off on him.

James ordered a coffee and a sandwich and joined me at the table. 'There's a big thaw on,' he said. 'It's meant to rain for the next couple of days. Do you want me to take those snowshoes back home with me after I get back to Glenfinnan? You won't need them any more. Winter's gone.'

'What do you mean by gone?'

He took a bite from his sandwich and spread his hands. 'MWIS say it's going to be fifteen degrees at sea level by this time next week. The long-range forecast is for gales, rain and rapid thaw. I doubt you'll see much winter from now on.'

My inner pessimist wasn't surprised. This, after all, was usual for backpacking in Scotland – but not in mid-February.

'This was supposed to be a winter trip,' I grumbled into my coffee. 'It feels more like October so far.'

'I think this is the new normal, to be honest,' James said.

***

We stood next to his car in the sluicing rain as we faffed with rucksacks and gear. I unclipped the bulky blue snowshoes that had been lashed to the sides of my pack for days, taking care not to snag the straps on those sharp metal teeth, and dumped them in the boot on top of a pile of my brother's climbing and camera gear. Then I dug the faulty tent out of the top of my pack. Its stuffsack felt damp, and the whole package felt heavy in that absorbed-loads-of-water kind of way. I couldn't wait to be rid of it.

The spare tent James now handed to me was about half the packed size and half the weight of the faulty one. It was a basic pyramid-shaped shelter that would work well in high winds, and it pitched using my trekking poles combined together as a support. I'd also asked Hannah to send up my bivvy bag and groundsheet. I worried about whether this shelter set-up would be robust enough for hardcore winter conditions, but I had little choice – it was the only other tent I had available that would be up to the job. I stuffed the package into my rucksack.

James passed me the supply box he'd brought up from his home on the Black Isle, and I opened it with my penknife. Inside I found the food and supplies I'd need to keep me going for the next fifty miles until Shiel Bridge. There were cereal and chocolate bars, dehydrated meal packs and, most importantly, the first of four monster payloads of Soreen malt loaf. Malt loaf resists being frozen and is the cheapest way to pack 800 calories into something I can stomach day after day for weeks. When I'd bought my malt loaf in the Skegness Tesco superstore, I'd cleared the shelves – and astonished the girl at the checkout.

***

In my mind, the Bealach Allt n' Chaoruinn had always marked the symbolic entry point to Knoydart, and the watershed beyond which the character of the Cape Wrath Trail changes dramatically.

We climbed up to the pass in heavy rain, fording the burn a few times where it foamed over the track. Streams sluiced down the slopes on both sides, leaping from tussock to tussock where there had been unbroken snow the day before. A few sad snow patches remained. I bent down to get a close look at one of them. Its softening mass slumped and drooped and dripped. Green pillows of moss beneath it looked more vivid than I had expected in that faded landscape of yellow and brown, as if nourished by the droplets it received from the dying snow that shielded it from the rain above.

On the other side of the pass, the landscape opened up to reveal a broad glen with a meandering river at the bottom of it leading into Knoydart. I could see a few solitary trees clinging to the banks of a ravine. Every wrinkle and fold in the landscape was laid bare to scrutiny, and the mountains in the distance looked almost entirely clear of snow. The path continued towards the river beneath us, but I knew that soon the path would grow faint before vanishing altogether on this side of the river.

The first major river crossing on the Cape Wrath Trail with no bridge or ford lay just ahead of us. It was not *the* crossing – the Carnach crossing that I had fretted over for so long lay many miles to the north-west – but it was the first real test.

'We'll need to find the best place to cross the river,' I said to James as we paused for a moment, munching snacks. I pointed about a mile downstream with a trekking pole. 'There's usually a good spot somewhere over there, but I'm a bit concerned about how high the river looks, what with all this rain.'

James nodded. He was carrying a blue Osprey rucksack only just large enough for his hiking and camping gear, and there was an extra dry bag strapped to the left-hand side above the huge camera bag swinging from a strap across his body, giving him a lopsided look.

The weather had begun to clear just in time for the rough descent towards the ravine. Light scurried over the hillside. I watched James as his gaze scanned the landscape, and I recognised that look, alert and precise – he was seeking photographic opportunities. In moments my brother had his DSLR in both hands, scouting out possible images. A professional landscape and wildlife photographer, James had decided to join me as far as A'Chuil bothy for two reasons: first to enjoy a taste of Cape Wrath Trail life with me, and second to carry out a paying job. I needed images for my magazine articles, and good ones. Editors look for images with human interest, and it is remarkably difficult to photograph yourself when hiking alone – at least, it's difficult to do it well. A tripod, self-timer and a little patience will do the job, but the results are rarely anything better than adequate. I'd decided to hire James for a couple of days. His talent with lens and light would significantly boost the quality of what I could offer to my editor.

'Let's get a shot of you walking in front of that snow patch down there,' James said. He'd swapped lenses and was pacing to and fro, gaze locked on the middle distance, gauging perspective.

Time to get to work. I let James do his job, and carried out his instructions, often climbing back uphill to cross the same patch of ground again and again while James tried different angles and compositions. I didn't mind – this was part of why we were both here. But it did reinforce the fact that the demands of work still had a hold of me, even in this place, on the very threshold of Knoydart's outer realm.

We hiked downhill. When in the mountains together, I naturally fell into place behind James. Despite being the younger brother by three years, he had significantly more experience in the Scottish mountains; he'd climbed twice as many Munros as I had, and spent a good chunk of his working life guiding clients in wild places like the Monadhliath and the Cairngorms, seeking mountain hares and other creatures to photograph. The mountains were his life. He'd started out as a hillwalker like me before becoming obsessed with solo climbing – a relationship that turned sour when it ended up intensifying his depression and anorexia during a bad phase of his life. He'd found solace in wildlife photography and, perversely, caving. Although the shadow of depression would never leave him, James was a different man now, more at ease with himself and more willing to own his successes than he had been in his twenties.

As we walked, I constantly scanned the river for possible crossing places. I couldn't quite remember where I'd forded it on my last visit in December. A little further downstream, perhaps – but water levels had been much lower earlier in the winter, and now an angry torrent boiled through the ravine, scouring the banks and covering rapids in white spray.

'I think we need to get across soon,' James said. 'If we keep descending it's going to be impossible. Look at it.'

A few minutes later, we saw two camo-clad estate workers, one carrying a rifle in a protective cover, and a third driving an all-terrain Argocat, descending parallel to us on the other side of the river. We waved to them, and they stopped to wave back. They seemed to confer amongst themselves for a moment and then we heard a shout above the roar of the river: 'CROSS HERE! CROSS HERE!'

I looked at James. He nodded, and cupped his mouth to shout back: 'OK, THANKS!'

The man in front gave us a thumbs up, and they kept going.

'I guess we're crossing here, then,' I said, looking down the steep boggy slope to the river below us. I wasn't too happy with being told where to cross, but the estate workers must know what the river was like further downstream.

James pointed. 'Just down there. It flattens out a bit. Doesn't look too bad.'

When we reached the bank, we both stood there looking at the river for a few moments. It was no more than a few metres to the other side. The crossing didn't actually look that bad, but appearances could be deceptive, and the current was still flowing fast and strong.

'I'll go first,' James said; then, with a mischievous grin, 'I'll get a cool shot of you wading across. Might ask you to do it twice if I don't get it the first time.'

I looked at my watch. 'Three hours. Not bad for Scotland.'

'What?' he said, hovering on the bank.

'That's how long we've managed to keep our feet dry today. Hope you've packed your towel.'

He made me wade the river three times in all. The water was freezing at first, although as it poured into my boots and sloshed around my toes, finding its way over the cuffs of my knee-height waterproof socks and spreading downwards, it soon warmed up. After a few minutes my boots felt as if they had been packed with jelly. On the far bank I poured the water from each boot and laced them back on tightly again.

I couldn't help but notice that James was looking a bit too pleased with himself for someone who had just waded across a river as cold as that one.

'What?' I said.

'My feet feel pretty dry, actually. These winter boots are fantastic.' He pointed to his massive orange mountaineering boots with built-in gaiters – the sort of thing you'd wear on Mont Blanc.

'You git.'

***

Hours later, we came to the forestry track that would lead us into Glen Dessarry and to our bothy for the night. The forest we entered was not the vibrant wildwood that filled my dreams, but a commercial plantation. Tall spruces crammed together coated these hillsides. Boughs rippled above in unfelt breezes. At our feet, ferns gestured towards the light, while the living strata of mosses concealed all that might lie beneath, along with the muffling drape of spruce needles. Distantly, the *peep, peep* of a bird echoed through those strange corridors to our ears, a signpost amidst the silence.

Timber crops have a certain weird aura all of their own. I grew up in woods like these. Tunstall Forest, on the Suffolk coast, was my haunt as a teenager, and I grew to recognise its watchful quiet, its sudden sighs, the ultra-compressed density of its birch thickets – a folding and forging of space into something denser, layered, and new. Such woods seem to contain more space and time than could be rationally accounted for.

Perhaps the greatest sin of the commercial timber crop is that it is a destroyer of place. Much has been lost to the plantations, smothered beneath the pine needles, prised apart by probing roots. An annihilation of memory. In Knoydart, a place of fading echoes and voices, this entombment could feel all the more stifling.

Above us, mist-cloaked mountains rose drab and grey into the darkening sky. Although my watch said it was mid-afternoon I knew that night wouldn't be far away. We strode along the broad track side by side, trekking poles clicking.

'So what's it been like?' James asked me after a while. 'No internet, I mean.'

His question didn't surprise me. It had been an unspoken question since we'd met up earlier that day, pushed aside by more immediately pressing concerns. I had known he'd be curious, because we'd spoken about what I planned to do many times. What surprised me was how little the question seemed to matter in this place. Knoydart itself was a sort of vast Walden Zone – an area of no phone signal, unless you climbed high enough to catch a bar or two of scrappy 2G. Going offline here was easier than in most other places in the British Isles, but I'd hardly even thought about it. In a way I was a little disappointed. I had wanted some kind of grand revelation. It was hard to admit that this particular Walden Zone might just be a big patch of bog where I couldn't tweet.

'I've only been offline for seven days,' I said, then realised that I was try-ing to dodge the question because it was harder than I thought it would be. 'I think I expected it to be a bigger deal than it really is, at least so far. Do you know what I mean?'

'Aye, maybe,' James said. 'But when's the last time you were completely offline for a week? Nobody ever is these days.'

I thought back. It had been an embarrassingly long time. I'd been a smartphone user since 2010. Even before then, on long trips to the moun-tains I'd usually gravitated towards an internet café after a few days for checking emails and posting updates to Facebook.

'2005, I think,' I said eventually. 'That big backpacking trip to the Lake District. Twenty days with no smartphone and no emails.'

He chuckled. 'I remember Mum going a bit nuts because she hadn't heard from you in ages. That was quite a low-stress trip, wasn't it? Not like this one.'

'That's a fair point. The logistics have been challenging. I've had a lot to think about.' I paused. 'The only time when I really felt the need for the internet – or at least the comfort of connection – was in Salen, at the B&B. Off trail.'

'And out here it doesn't seem to matter?'

'In fact, the whole circus is starting to feel strange,' I replied. 'Have you ever stopped to think about how weird Twitter is? This mad website where people scroll for hours and compete with each other for the attention of strangers, for fleeting points on some scale nobody even understands, and get angry for no reason. It all seems so important at the time, Twitter and email and the news and everything else, but step away for a few days and it just seems weird and shouty and irrelevant to anything that might be important.' I spread my arms to the encircling forest. 'There seems to be so much that we need to care about and have an opinion on, but maybe there isn't. Maybe there's nothing more to it all than this.'

I stopped my little rant mid-flow, surprised at myself. I'd articulated thoughts I didn't even know I'd had. Maybe I was learning something – or at least feeling something – after all.

***

We finished the last couple of kilometres in near-darkness. As we'd strolled along the easy, undulating trail, chatting and putting the world to rights, neither of us had noticed that we were getting a bit tired and hadn't been drinking as much as we should. We got out our head torches and filled up our bottles at the stream before completing the final descent to A'Chuil in the dark, down a steep muddy trail that slithered along a firebreak between the stream and a wall of conifers. Suddenly, the night seemed absolute. I switched my torch on.

A low ruined wall topped with moss appeared in my torch beam, and I looked up to see another wall behind it and the slates of the bothy roof. I wasn't looking forward to a stay in this bothy. A'Chuil had seemed a damp and unfriendly place on my last visit. This time, however, it greeted us as a haven. After exploring the interior, we settled on the left-hand room, where a large sleeping platform offered plenty of space to lay out our sleeping pads. I lit a few candles to chase away the darker shadows in the corners. While James hung up his sodden waterproofs on the clothes line hanging near the window, I set to work boiling water. My stomach growled. We'd both walked fourteen miles that day over rough terrain, and I hadn't taken in enough calories.

When I glanced back at James, he was balancing an off-camera flash-gun on a miniature tripod, and looked up with a grin in response to my questioning look.

'Great opportunity for some images in the candlelight. You're doing a comparative review of all those dehydrated backpacking meals, aren't you? An image of you preparing one on your stove could look pretty good.'

He set up the shot. It felt surreal. I'd been out on the hill with James in hired pro photographer mode before, so I'd had an idea of what to expect, but somehow it still surprised me – that even at seven o'clock at night in a bothy in the middle of nowhere, with a stomach no doubt demanding to be fed as urgently as mine was, his mind was still at least partly in work mode, seeking images. If I needed another reminder that this journey was a gear in the machine of the outdoor economy, here it was.

Afterwards, as we sat on mismatched bothy furniture scooping spoonfuls of hot rehydrated mush into our mouths, the map laid out on the table in front of us, James said something that made me realise how out of touch I'd become with the subtle world of winter mountain conditions. As an obsessive climber years before, when I'd lived in Glen Coe and could see the mountains out of my bedroom window, I'd kept such a close eye on weather patterns and snow reports that I had a pretty good idea at any point during the winter what conditions would be like at various altitudes and slope aspects. This is life-saving information. Know what has happened to the snow and you can learn to predict hazards, but building up this knowledge takes both experience and close attention. While I had plenty of experience, there's only so much attention you can pay to a developing Scottish winter season when you live down south in England, and perhaps I'd lost the knack.

All those thoughts sprinted through my mind after I heard James say this: 'Are you sure you want to head over that bealach given what the snow's been doing? A north-facing slope at that altitude is going to be dodgy if you ask me.'

I thought about what we'd seen that day: rapid thaw and a disappearing snow line. Then I thought about my crossing of Bealach Coire nan Gall during my Knoydart recce trip back in December, standing at that high, lonely col looking down the ribbon of the river over steep crags that, right now, might be holding a sagging weight of snow just waiting to avalanche. Perhaps an overhanging cornice. Why hadn't I been thinking about that?

So much depended on the Knoydart section of the trail. Fail here and I'd fail hard, but if I could push through, make it to Kinloch Hourn, my chances of completing the CWT would be significantly boosted. I'd been thinking about the river crossings. I'd been thinking about the freezing, thigh-deep crossing of the Finiskaig, about that missing bridge over the Carnach. I'd been thinking, frankly, like a summer backpacker would, but at this time of year there were more hazards to consider, and perhaps my planning hadn't been comprehensive enough.

'Well,' I said, unsure how to explain my own lack of care, 'I was thinking that most of the snow would have gone.'

James reached over and drew the map closer to him. 'Facing north at 700 metres? Probably not.'

'Do you think I should risk the river crossing, then?'

'Put it this way,' James said after another mouthful of pasta, 'you've got two options. Cross two rivers, one of which you're familiar with, or risk getting avalanched on a steep bealach you've never even seen in winter conditions, miles from anywhere.'

'When you put it like that ... '

'If it was me, there's no way I'd risk a route like that after this much snow and a rapid thaw. Also, there are more gales forecast.'

I didn't add that I had a third option: retreat back to Glenfinnan. But that wasn't really an option. I'd known that I'd face difficult decisions on this journey. Making those difficult decisions was one reason why I was doing this. Like Thoreau in *Walden,* I wanted to live deliberately – to own my choices. Part of being cut off from the hive mind of the internet was to be intentional and learn to listen to my own thoughts again. To trust my instincts and abilities. It's so easy to assume that every problem has already been solved and recorded in the global ledger of the World Wide Web, but out in the mountains there are real choices, real consequences, and I had chosen not to allow myself the comfort of a quick Google search to figure out what I should do – even if I had the signal. It was all about digging deep in my own experience and trusting the people I was with.

Had I already failed at that? Why had I been so blind to the avalanche risk of my chosen escape route? I'd been so focused on the river crossings I feared that I had completely failed to think about what was happening to the snow. Was I too soft, too digital, for this hard analogue Walden Zone I now had to survive in?

'Looks like I'll be crossing the Carnach, then,' I said after a while.

James shrugged. 'Look on the bright side.' He hesitated. 'I'm sure you'll think of one.'

***

Day 8: 13 February 2019

The forest enfolded us in silence as we struggled through the bogs and the mud. Above the treetops, I could hear gusts tearing past, whipping the pine boughs into a frenzy, but down here beside the river all was calm – and mild. James had stopped to take his fleece off about half an hour ago and now trudged a few metres ahead with his waterproof jacket zipped up against the drizzle.

'It feels like summer, doesn't it?' he said after a while. 'You almost expect a cloud of midges to descend.'

He was right. Damp, mild but not warm, and hardly a trace of snow visible anywhere – this felt like June. In fact, for an eerie moment I felt myself drop back through time to land on this very spot in June 2015, during my first Cape Wrath Trail. Conditions had been almost identical. If anything, it had probably been colder then.

Winter's gone, James had told me, and I hadn't wanted to believe him. But he'd been right.

The path was as nasty as I remembered it. The word 'path' might conjure up an image of a decent trail where you can put one foot in front of the other, but I'd found that Knoydart paths often resembled nightmarish quagmires filled with a morass of green slime and bottomless black pools. Because nobody ever wanted to walk right through the middle, the edges of these paths inevitably expanded as people sought drier ground. But in Knoydart nowhere was dry, and in places people had veered five or ten metres from the track to find easier ways around particularly nasty pools, only to end up churning up any firm ground that might once have existed. Following a Knoydart bog-path usually took at least twice as long as expected.

Eventually we climbed out of the woodland and, after passing a broken deer fence rotting into the peat, emerged on to the open hillside. The contrast between dense, moss-draped conifer plantation below and bare landscape above was striking. There was no gradual, sympathetic merging of habitats. The landscape beyond the fence was absolutely barren. Out-croppings of dark rock, looking almost black in the feeble morning light, poked through the russet carpet of deer grass. The full force of the wind howled down on us from the heights, and I could see vast ripples spreading through the grass like waves on an undulating sea.

James peered up into the murk, tracing the stream of the Allt a' Bhealaich as it leapt between small scrappy buttresses on its way down from Bealach Coire nan Gall 500 metres above us. That was the alternative route through Knoydart I had so painstakingly planned and reconnoitred – my way of avoiding the fear of the Carnach river crossing. I'd poured so much anxiety and hope into this nondescript patch of hillside that this seemed like a significant moment as we stood at the turning point beneath it. I had already made the choice, but it was not yet made real. I knew that what I did now could change not only my life but the lives of everyone I loved, everyone I worked with, everyone I might ever meet or talk to.

On the other hand, maybe it was only a hill. Maybe all this time, all this mental freedom, was encouraging my tendency to overthink things. Maybe the choice was not really a choice at all.

'I think it's time for me to head back to the car,' James said. 'There's a blister niggling at my heel, and I don't want it to get any worse – I've got a lot of wildlife guiding coming up.'

His talk of mundane things jolted me back to the here and now. 'Will you stop at the bothy again overnight? You could always spend the night at Corryhully.'

He'd taken his map out and was studying it. 'Actually I reckon I'll power through and see if I can get all the way back to Glenfinnan tonight.'

That surprised me, but James was extremely fit. 'OK.' Suddenly I didn't want him to go. I loved walking alone, but I never spent enough time walking with my brother, and these moments tended to feel more valuable in retrospect. 'Thanks for walking with me.'

'No bother,' he said with a grin. 'It's been fun, getting a taste of life on the Cape Wrath Trail. Listen – are you going to promise me you won't head up over the bealach? The rivers will be fine, honestly. It hasn't rained that much, and the rivers weren't too high this morning, were they? Just don't risk it.'

'I promise.'

He hiked back the way we had come.

***

My apprehension followed me, although there was also a sense of freedom as I climbed up into the mist, following the foaming line of the Allt a' Ghiubhais through the bogs and tussocks, the weather turning wetter and wilder with every step. I'd forgotten how rough the ground was here, how the path would be clear one moment and then gone the next. It took longer than I expected to reach Lochan a' Mhaim, a flat grey expanse of water hunkered down beneath mountains that still held on to flecks of their snow cover. On a clear day in autumn, I'd been told, this was a place with that gleam of Knoydart magic about it, but I'd never been here on a clear day.

I soon passed the spot where, almost four years before, a gust of wind had knocked my tent flat in the middle of the night and I'd woken amongst a tangle of nylon and guyropes. Tense minutes had followed as I tried to keep my gear dry while gust after gust tore over the water, howling like vengeful monsters before smashing against me in volleys of freezing rain. Mountain storms have a way of putting the human animal back in its place. It's easy to believe in the animate, wilful power of nature at such times, even if only for an instant.

After passing through a bottleneck in the landscape where knurled jaws of rock reached out from the mountains and pinched the lochan shut, the valley opened out once again and the river was released from its constraints to meander at will through a meadow. The crag I'd passed beneath was called Creag an Taghain – the cliff of the pine marten. A few birches clung high on the rocks, trembling in the sleet. I wondered if any pine martens still lived there.

I approached the second major river crossing of the Cape Wrath Trail. The river broadened, slowed and dug deeper as it rounded another curve.

Now the Finiskaig ford lay directly ahead of me. It didn't look anywhere near as bad as I had expected after the incessant rain and melting snow – in fact, I was struck by the quietness of the river as it whispered over the shoals of stones it had collected in its bed. I had expected rolling white water here, a fearsome wade braced against trekking poles as I fought the living pressure of the river, but instead the water no more than nudged at my calves when I stepped into the current. The chill of cold water sloshing in my boots reminded me that this was something real, an experience in a place without bridges, but the river hadn't even been knee deep.

If the Finiskaig was this easy, maybe the Carnach would be easy too. Maybe I'd been worrying all this time for nothing.

***

The last mile to Sourlies never seemed to come to an end as I trudged down the steep and rocky path, trying to skirt the bogs, drawn onwards by the view of Loch Nevis in the distance. At the kinloch where the river emptied itself into this great sea fjord, a cluster of roofless ruins marked one of the many settlements of old Knoydart. Now nobody lived there. The last building with a roof stood hunched against the hillside a little way further. Sourlies had once been the site of a whisky house, where folk came from all over the area to drink – illegally at various times in Scotland's history – and swap news and stories.

Now it is a bothy maintained by the Mountain Bothies Association. A roof of corrugated iron keeps out the weather, while the thick drystone walls keep in the warmth. I approached in the gathering gloom of mid-afternoon, stepping over banded drifts of orange bladderwrack that waves and tide had deposited high up the hindshore's close-cropped grass. Outside the bothy, I dumped my pack and opened the door; inside was dark, lit only dimly by the roof skylight. There were sleeping platforms, a table with a few odds and ends – old gas canisters, plastic bottles, cigarette lighters, glass jars, packets of mouse-nibbled Super Noodles – and a tiny fireplace in the wall at the far end, which was blackened with soot. Above the fireplace, my gaze was met by the eternal stare of the Watcher of Sourlies: a ram's skull of impressive size with two spiral horns, suspended above an ancient hand-carved wooden plaque that read 'SOURLIES BOTHY'. The plaque was as grimed by soot as the wall it adorned.

I nodded to the skull. 'Afternoon.'

It occurred to me then that Sourlies was an island, at least as far as the Cape Wrath Trail was concerned, pinned between the fords of the Finiskaig and Carnach with no easy way in or out that did not involve crossing water. An inaccessible place within an inaccessible place. A fortified inner citadel, or perhaps a buried acorn.

The Watcher watched me as I stood there, struck still by this idea. I wondered how long that skull had hung on the wall. Certainly since my first Cape Wrath Trail in 2015, but not, I suspected, looking at the condition of the skull, that much longer. Within recent memory it had been a living being that had roamed the hills, learnt how to move over crag and scree, felt the cold and the rain, seen the sweep of colours over the loch, lived with others of its kind. Then it had died, and in its afterlife it had become the warden of this strange and isolated place – in essence if not if any practical sense. Sourlies itself, perhaps, mirrored the journey of this traveller. It was only then that I noticed the half-full whisky bottle glinting in the pool of diffuse light on the table. Centuries ago people had met here for strong booze and stronger bonds; now the community it serves is flung far, but perhaps it fulfils the same role as it ever did.

***

Day 9: 14 February 2019

A light breeze blew all night, sneaking under the flysheet of my tent pitched outside the bothy and somehow, improbably, drying out the wet socks that I'd draped over my boots. By the time I came to strike camp the next morning, I could hear a constant fine drizzle pattering on the fabric. Mist hung low over the loch as I walked along the beach above the tideline and then climbed up and over the headland of Strone

Sourlies – a place where the trail completely disappeared and, for about half a kilometre, I was on my own.

At the crest of the headland, as I fought my way through brittle old bracken, I looked down and beheld the estuary and river plain of the Carnach.

There were mudflats and salt marshes to my left, beyond the knoll of Eilean Tioram – a landscape that reminded me of the flat coastal landscapes of Suffolk where I'd spent so much time as a teenager, where Dad's boat *Yorrel* had once rested at anchor. Upriver, I saw the place where the rickety old bridge over the Carnach had once stood. It had been the sort of bridge that makes you wonder if you'll make it across without it snapping in half. The bridge had finally been removed in 2017 after having been declared too dangerous to use. Nobody knew when the replacement would be installed. This fact had been the cause of a good chunk of my anxiety before and during this trip, and now I'd come face to face with my nemesis river crossing.

I thought back to all my planning and preparation, to my recce trip through Knoydart the previous year, all to avoid the threat of the missing bridge. I thought back to standing at Bealach Coire nan Gall and feeling anxiety tear at me. This moment was the summit of all those other moments.

I approached the bank of the river where the bridge once stood. Rusty iron stumps and bits of rotting railway sleeper protruded from the pile of rocks that had once anchored the bridge to the earth. The river didn't look like much – just a few metres to the other side, but the current was fast and strong, and the far bank was steeper than it looked. This was not a good place to cross. I decided to hike a little way upstream, keeping an eye on the river to my left as I sloshed through the marshy terrain.

Much sooner than I had expected, the Carnach broadened into a gentle, shallow course that looked trivial to cross. Surely it could not be this easy? I stood on the bank and scrutinised the river. Water babbled over a flat bed of small pebbles. I could clearly see all the way to the bottom – it looked no more than a foot deep, and there were no hidden drops, pools, or rapids. This was the place.

After adjusting my gaiters, I stepped down from the mossy bank and into the Carnach. It felt almost forbidden. After the stories of hikers being drowned trying to cross this river, it hardly seemed decent that I should be able to cross this easily – as if there should be more of a sense of occasion. But it was as easy as it looked. Easier than the Finiskaig. The water hardly came over my ankles, and by the time I climbed out on to the far bank I felt as if I'd found a secret shortcut through time and space.

***

Memories are not photographs. They're more like cryptic runes, weathered in place on a stone slab after hundreds of years, their meaning decipherable but lacking context. Data, not meaning – that's how memories all too often are for me. I think I have remembered a place's essence until I return there and realise that my memories are nothing more than shadows of reality.

As I walked along the left bank of the Carnach, I realised that I'd largely forgotten the mythic grandeur of Knoydart's innermost realm. Mountain walls of impossible ruggedness rose from the gorge of the river, their flanks bristling with black rock, while birch, holly and oak overarched the rapids. These trees felt like priceless jewels to me as I walked beneath gnarled trunks that bore the scars of time, weather, and more than a few woodpeckers. Ancient birches more dead than alive rose from the thick carpet of moss covering the car-sized boulders strewn over the hillside to my left. The moss extended for a metre or more up their trunks in places, and it was impossible to tell where rock, moss or tree began or ended.

This living wood had once carpeted much of Knoydart – an Atlantic rainforest of extraordinary richness and beauty, harvested hundreds of years ago for shipbuilding and firewood. The fragments that remain have a certain aura. A tangible awareness can be felt in these very special refuges. Species of animals and plants persist here that have vanished elsewhere. Others remain as ghosts of yearning, after-images in the mind, almost but not quite forgotten by the collective store of memory – the lynx, the wolf, the bear, the elk, surviving now only in a scatter of Gaelic place names. These woods may be diminished, and most of them may be ageing into senility as grazing pressure from deer prevents any regeneration, but to walk through such a place is to feel the glow and the glory of non-human life. It's a reminder that the real world is not the smooth, streamlined, cynical machine of capitalism and the internet and human concerns, and all the other terribly important stuff we fill our time with. The real world is moss and bark and mud and the puff of a robin's breath condensing in the air at dawn.

I stood there and stared at a rowan climbing out of the cleft in a boulder. The patterns of green and grey on its trunk looked like constellations.

Reality is what one pays attention to. When all I'd been paying attention to were Twitter and emails and my endless to-do list, reality was a fractured whirlpool. All that hardly even seemed real now. The very fabric of the universe had changed. My mind felt like a different thing – no longer an algorithm or a shard of the machine, more like a river-washed stone. My thoughts felt slower and less frayed, less multithreaded. Was this a permanent change? Was it really a change at all?

After fighting through a dense tangle of forest between the mountain wall and the torrent, I came upon a place that I did remember from my 2015 CWT. The gorge opened out and the river widened into a deep, silent pool directly beneath a black cliff face at least ten metres high. Saplings and heather and ferns clung to the ledges and cracks in the rock, and the pool below was transparent and still, its clarity so perfect that it seemed to luminesce. The meadow cupped in this cradle between forest and fell tugged at something deep in my soul. It was a perfect pocket meadow – a place where, two centuries or more ago, a family would have rested at dusk on a summer evening after tending their cattle, a home-spun picnic rug spread out between the flowers, children laughing and skimming stones in the pool while their mother whistled at the birds and fireflies darted between the birches. There was a miniature tumbledown ruin in the centre of the meadow – just a curve of drystone wall capped with moss, a young rowan sprouting from its centre. A summer shieling, no doubt, but human beings had once slept there and woken there, watched the stars turn from this tiny scrap of the universe.

It was silent now. Most of Knoydart's people were long gone. The ancient roads through this land were trodden now only by the deer, the people who cared for the deer and paid to shoot the deer, and other people like me who walked through and wondered at the meaning of names like Cnoc Allt na Seilge and Mam Unndalain – names rich with culture and memory now almost forgotten. Though a few others had come to settle here, drawn by the wildness and the beauty, its population was a fraction of what it had once been.

Magic still fizzed in that place, but it was a sad magic, tinged with all that had been lost. Tinged with hopefulness too, of course, for if Knoydart is an island then it is also a lifeboat. Rewilding projects on the Knoydart peninsula hope to bring back native forest and wildlife. The John Muir Trust has owned 3,000 acres of land on Knoydart for decades, and life is returning.

I didn't linger in the meadow. It felt like a sacred, guarded place that my presence would somehow taint. I walked on, marvelling that although I had remembered the existence of the meadow and the ruin, their meaning had been mine to rediscover.

Is the feebleness of memory a curse or a gift? I think it is a gift. If all memories were recorded in perfect three-dimensional colour, emotion and experience available to sample at any time, experiences could never be relived or renewed.

***

The high pass of Mam Unndalain wasn't windy for once, and the cloud began to clear as I descended the other side. Views opened up over hillsides where scraggly new birch forests huddled behind deer fences. After a rough descent of Gleann Unndalain's narrow slot between rocky mountain walls, following the churning river and its many cataracts, I caught a glimpse of Barrisdale Bay a couple of kilometres north. Clustered near the shore, I knew, were a few houses, a campsite and a bothy. I wasn't out of the area of zero mobile reception yet, but I'd passed through Knoydart's core – the area I thought of as most remote, most challenging, most wild.

The bothy, a small outbuilding next to a farm, was locked up when I passed it. I found somewhere to camp just a few hundred metres along the gravel track running next to the salt marsh at the loch's margins. A strip of dry, soft grass extended like a runway into the estuary, and I pitched my tent there above the high-tide line, luxuriating in the fact that I could leave gear out on the grass without it getting soaked by rain or blown away. Up went the tent as the light faded.

Clouds had fled the sky, leaving only a high haze that scattered the blue hour and cast a delicate brilliance over the land. I spent ten minutes watching the stars wink above Ladhar Bheinn's summit snowfields, which were all aglow, as if they alone retained the last embers of the dying sun and now radiated it back into the night. Gathered around me were the sounds of the sea loch: waves lapping on the shore, the occasional honk of geese, the nostalgic, warbling, haunting gleam of a curlew. It was utterly calm. I felt at peace, anxiety ebbing as low as the tide, and yet in a strange way I felt closer to my dad in that place, at that moment. I thought about the curlews that flitted over the mudflats of the Suffolk estuaries, and I realised at once that the solitude in nature I so valued is an oxymoron anyway – there are always other creatures watching and listening, carrying out their own full and dramatic lives all around. Sparks of awareness and emotion. We aren't separate from nature. We're never alone.

He would have loved this so much.

Chapter 6

Somewhere to my left there was a huffing sound. I heard it distinctly over the rhythmic murmur of the wavelets coming in off the loch and splashing against the shore. I looked and there was an otter floating there in the swell, surrounded by garlands of drifting bladderwrack, its blunt little whiskered nose pointing in my direction. It blinked and huffed again.

The otter watched me for a few seconds more and then dived. I hadn't had time to get my camera out of its bag, but now I stood there with camera at the ready, waiting for it to surface again. When it popped its head back above the surface, closer to me this time, it was soon joined by two other individuals. The three floating otter heads bobbed there not five metres away; they looked quizzically up at me, then they each glanced at each other, as if seeking a consensus on whether this strange backpack-toting stranger was a threat or a friend. The first one huffed for a third time and they all dived.

As I walked on along the shore path I kept looking down at the water, hoping to see the otters again. Sure enough, after a few minutes I saw the three otters surfacing once more; they'd followed me underwater, and now paddled along on the surface, keeping pace with my strides. They dived. They surfaced again. Sometimes I saw all three, but more often it was just one animal – the first, I imagined, although to my untrained eye all three looked alike. I wondered how I looked to them.

The shoreline path from Barrisdale to Kinloch Hourn was a route I had walked several times before. It was the shortest stage of the Cape

Wrath Trail, but on my first CWT I'd found it surprisingly tough thanks to the atrocious weather. This time there was a lot less water cascading down the hillsides and I even had the side zips of my Páramo trousers open for ventilation in the warm conditions.

I didn't stop at Kinloch Hourn. This tiny cluster of houses at the head of the loch is the location of the only public telephone on the Knoydart section of the CWT, but it had been out of action for months, ever since a landslide had wiped out a section of road – along with the phone line – in November 2018. I'd tried to use it on my trip in December, but the ancient phone wouldn't take my coins, and soon a camo-clad stalker had pulled up in his six-wheeled ATV and cheerfully told me that all communications with the outside world had been cut off. I chuckled as I remembered his gleeful rant about the inefficiency of the Highland Council. Just before this trip I'd found out that plans to fix the road (and the phones) were due to get going 'at about Easter'. Perhaps the Knoydart Walden Zone had a way of defending itself, reinforcing its seclusion, but one person's digital detox is someone else's disrupted livelihood. I couldn't imagine having a conversation with the stalker about the healing value of time spent in seclusion away from the internet. We lived in different worlds, and that was fine.

At 699 metres above sea level, Bealach Coire Mhalagain is the highest point on the regular line of the CWT. That's well below most of the summits nearby, but high enough that I'd lost some sleep over it during the planning phase. In summer it's an exposed notch between mountain peaks, with plenty of rough, off-path walking on both sides of the col. I'd found the descent particularly tricky on my first CWT. Steep ground combined with compass-in-hand navigation is a recipe for caution at any time of year, but in winter, when the north-east-facing bealach would probably be banked out with snow, perhaps even corniced, it represented a major challenge. Any steep, hard snow on the far side would require ice axe and crampons. Despite the intensity of the recent thaw, I expected to find at least some snow lurking on the other side.

The warmth of the afternoon surprised me. It was feeling a lot like spring. With my increased pace on this section I started to feel that familiar pull of bigger miles and sunnier trails – a rising of the hiker's sap that I feel every year, usually from around March or April. It's a transformation as inexorable as the metamorphosis of caterpillar to moth, or the unfurling of hawthorn buds. Invariably I dust off the box labelled 'ultra-light gear' and start dreaming about big days in rugged Alpine landscapes with the sun beating down on me. I had never felt this particular urge in February before. In February I was usually still fantasising about perfect winter conditions.

After the relative civilisation of Kinloch Hourn, the wilder expanse of Coire Mhalagain felt like an opportunity to breathe deeply again. The good path I'd been following disappeared at the river, and I struck uphill through a maze of moss-covered boulders and peat hags, keeping an eye on my map but not paying too much attention to navigation. To my left, white water foamed over cataracts, but water levels remained low, probably because most of the snow had now melted. Above, dun slopes rose to rockier heights where the summit of The Saddle (1,010 metres) hid somewhere behind the foreshortening perspective of snow-flecked crags. So little snow was left now that the latticework of white looked delicate and fragile, as if meticulously painted with the tiniest brush. Fine strokes of snow underlined cliffs and highlighted gullies, connecting a tenuous patchwork of blobs and shapes that would look different again in the morning after another twelve hours of hard melt. As I stood there and stared at this complex scene, more intricate than any drawing, I marvelled at the sequence of events – and blind entropy – that had led to its creation.

I wandered slowly uphill. The afternoon waned more quickly than I had expected, and with the fading of the light came the cloud, spreading from one corner of the sky to cover me with a uniform blanket of grey. Suddenly the warmth was gone and with it the fleeting sense of springlike promise. It had been an illusion – or perhaps a premonition. Time to find somewhere to camp and worry about Bealach Coire Mhalagain tomorrow.

***

The sound of rain drumming against the flysheet woke me with a start. I lay there motionless in my sleeping bag. Inches away from my face, I saw the fabric of my shelter leap and vibrate as if being pounded by an angry pianist. Somewhere in the distance, the storm growled – that deep, monstrous roar starting far away and gradually getting closer, rampaging over the landscape until it collided with my tent and I felt my shelter deform, thrashing to and fro, straining to deflect the gust.

Where the hell had this come from? I felt the anxiety burn. This had been one of my great fears on this trail: a winter storm that would chew me up and spit me out.

I sat upright in my sleeping bag, suddenly feeling constrained and alarmed. Blackness. I struggled to free an arm from my hood and grope for my head torch in the dark. The sudden beam, blinding me for a moment, cut through a haze of flying condensation droplets that had been shaken free from my flailing tent. I saw the central pole tilt and bend. In an instant I was hugging it, wrapping myself around it with both arms while I felt the gale moulding the tent's fabric to my body, pushing against me, an irresistible force. The mountain shrieked.

The cocktail of emotions coursing through me was one rarely to be experienced in our controlled and cosseted everyday lives. Near-religious awe of nature's power warred with a primal fear. Although I trusted my tent, trusted the strong central pole, trusted the tent pegs anchoring it to the ground, I'd rarely felt so exposed, so small. It does a person good to be reminded from time to time that they are no more than a speck – that ultimately nature is the boss.

Last time I'd camped high on a mountain in a storm, I remembered, the urge to plug myself back into the web and seek any comfort I could, any sense of connection at all, had been overwhelming. I'd flinched away from this mirror into my own soul. This time I looked for something within me to hold on to. I found it almost immediately.

The mythology of my childhood features a few particularly strong images. One is my dad's boat, *Yorrel*, that symbol of perfect solitude embedded within a landscape of both natural beauty and cocooning isolation. I thought back to all the stories, including the ones I'd told back to him at his deathbed. There had been storm as well as starlight.

The memory I held in my mind of him telling this story was one I couldn't be sure ever actually happened, but it was no less strong for all that. I remembered our living room at the old house in Caxton, where I'd lived for the first sixteen years of my life. I remembered the floral wallpaper, the heavy green curtains, and the old armchair in the corner that Dad used to sit in. Mum would be lying on the sofa reading a magazine. James would be playing with some Lego and I'd be sprawled on the carpet staring at the ceiling. The light in that room never seemed bright enough; it always felt like it was late evening, lit by the dim glow of electric lamps under heavy shades, or at least it did when I revisited it in my memories.

'Did I ever tell you and James about that time on the boat with the big storm?'

My ears pricked up. I'd heard the story before, of course, but I wanted to hear it again. I was probably about ten and therefore in a phase of being obsessed by boats and adventures on the water.

'Nope.'

I pictured my dad sitting in his chair – not my dad as he'd looked lying in hospital dying of cancer, but my dad as a much younger man. The default Ian Roddie as I always pictured him: about fifty years old, fit and sinewy, wearing old jeans and a pale blue shirt open at the collar, an unruly shock of black hair going white just above each ear, skin tanned from hours spent out in the garden. A sparkle in his eye that I would only much later recognise as gratitude.

'Well, it was October, and a gale blew in as they often did. I'd been on the boat for two days already. The wind was so strong that four-foot waves were hammering against the bow. I thought the boat was going to drag her anchor but she managed to stay put somehow. I went up on deck to secure the rigging. Madness up there – spray flying everywhere, waves breaking over the deck, could hardly see a thing.'

He smiled at me and James. Of course he knew that he'd told the story many times before, and that we wanted to hear it anyway.

'Just me and the boat, me and the storm. The noise was tremendous!

Like a jet engine going ahead. Then I *felt* something huge coming towards me. Still can't explain how I felt it before I saw it, but then there it was, a massive great big trimaran that had broken free of her moorings and was being tossed about in the swell like a rubber duck, coming straight towards me.'

James gasped, wide-eyed. The image of this huge, three-hulled boat loose and dangerous, driven by nothing but nature's energy, was illuminated as vividly in my mind as the pencil sketch Dad had drawn, years later, of *Yorrel* tilting in that same swell – a picture hanging framed on our living-room wall.

'It just went straight past, silent as a ghost, but enormous. I could have reached out and touched it. Nobody on board, of course, and it was gone in seconds. The next day it was found washed up on the mudflats.'

In my young mind, that storm had become *the* storm. All other storms I later read or heard about, all other storms I experienced myself, were subconsciously compared to that image of the flying trimaran and the lone mariner battling against the gale to secure his vessel. But perhaps, I realised, it was a naive and childish image of solitude. I loved the story, but perhaps I'd outgrown it.

I lay there in my sleeping bag, watching the tent buckle and bend around me in the light of my head torch, hearing the mountain scream and shout. I wondered if there was a monster out there, even now cannoning towards me, a loosed trimaran looking for a target. You couldn't control the uncontrollable. But just as my dad had trusted *Yorrel* completely, the yacht he had designed from scratch and built with his own hands, so I trusted my own ship moored fast in my own storm. I knew what I could rely on. I knew what I had to be anxious about and which worries were pointless.

What did solitude even mean? The concept had been reassuringly simple to me at the start of this trail, but it seemed complicated and full of questions now. Perhaps there was no such thing.

***

Day 11: 16 February 2019

It was a day of foaming burns and wind-driven spray, of fatigue, of wishing I were elsewhere.

Water preoccupied my thoughts as I slogged up to the bealach – how everything about my experience of hiking the Cape Wrath Trail was being shaped by water, how it was the dominant element, from the jewelled droplets on blades of grass to the unfathomable mass of the ever-present bog, from the artery network of burns to the thawing snowbeds. Briefly, I found myself visualising a mountain's water as more substantial than the rock, peat and vegetation. How would the mountain look without its water – desiccated, perhaps insubstantial as a shroud? How would the water look without the mountain?

The approach to the bealach looked familiar despite the poor visibility. I stuck to the right bank of a stream leaping in cascades down from mist above. When I reached the highest point, I found myself in a navigational quandary I remembered from my first CWT: follow the map, or the guidebook? I squinted at the map. It indicated that I should climb left and take a higher traversing line around the corrie rim. I looked in that direction. The ground was steep, rocky, and there were still some melting snowfields – although hardly more than the last time I'd been here, in June 2015. The guidebook said to descend and find a 'path of sorts'. From memory I knew that there wasn't much of a path at all for some distance on the other side of this nasty-looking drop.

I dithered, unable to choose between the two choices, although I already felt that the pressure was off. It may have been gusty and cold and wet, but the snow would have no effect on my progress. It could have looked very different – it *should* have looked very different. I was standing at the highest point on the Cape Wrath Trail in the middle of winter and I could barely see any snow.

An hour or two later, I found a scrap of phone signal on a prow of high ground above Glen Shiel. Below, through a veil of mist, I could see minute cars crawling along the ribbon of the road, but this evidence of the constructed world looked remote and insignificant from my vantage point.

Of more immediate impact were the two bars of 3G signal on my phone screen. This was a far more tangible indication that I'd made it through Knoydart's subtle aura – an aura that was all in my own head, but no less real because of it.

I phoned Hannah, and then my mum.

***

When I walked into the car park of the Kintail Lodge Hotel, Shiel Bridge, and dumped my backpack on the ground next to the door, I asked myself why things felt different. Younger versions of me had been to this place countless times before. It had always felt like a place between places rather than a destination or a beginning. For backpackers, mountain inns can often be like that. They are places where we can step aside from the flow of things for a little while and subconsciously reflect. Islands, perhaps, or safe havens to which we return between voyages.

I had last been here on 15 December the previous year after my Knoydart crossing. The place had looked dead from the outside, with no lights visible in any of the windows, but I found the door open and entered the bar to find it lit by a few candles and a cluster of locals supping their pints at the end of the bar. The power had been out for hours and the kitchen was shut. There were no other residents, and the staff seemed bored, but when I asked about a room and a meal they sprang into action.

That candlelit evening at the Kintail Lodge Hotel reminded me of the old days living and working at the Clachaig Inn in Glen Coe, when power cuts would bring out the best in everyone and the Clachaig would be transformed into a special, encapsulated world, insulated temporarily from everything outside. No internet, no TV, no artificial light – we'd drink beer in the flickering glow of a log fire, and the stories we'd weave would take on a richer, more honest, perhaps more vulnerable quality. But some magic is all the more valuable for being fleeting, and nobody would want to live that way forever if they had the choice.

Again I was the only resident staying at the hotel. Once I'd managed to track down a member of staff, I checked in and asked for my resupply box, secretly convinced that I'd receive nothing but a blank look and a 'What resupply box?' But there it was – that cardboard box filled with all the things I needed to keep me going for another sixty-five kilometres. I carried the box to my hotel room along with my pack, and there I luxuriated in gratitude for the simple, good things in life: a soft bed, a shower, somewhere to hang damp things up to dry, the certain knowledge that I had enough food to see me through to the next stage.

One stage at a time, I told myself. I'd made it this far, and only a short time ago I'd been convinced that I would quit. Cape Wrath still felt like a long way away, but Torridon didn't seem all that far, and that was the next step. *One stage at a time.*

Chapter 7

Day 12: 17 February 2019

> *Hi Alex. Good to hear you are making such good progress. I might join*
> *you when you get to Craig as the Torridon hills are some of my favourites.*
> *Weather not looking great for Monday. Talk soon.*

I'd received a text from Chris Townsend while tucking in to a plate of venison casserole in the lounge bar at the Kintail Lodge Hotel. My pub pitstop had been all about reconnection: phone conversations with family, phone conversations with friends, rapid-fire text messages from my brother relaying important weather information that I couldn't access myself because I wasn't using the internet, and simple, genuine in-person interactions with staff and fellow customers in the bar. After days by myself, these connections seemed to mean all the more, and I was thinking positive thoughts about the human race in general.

Part of the plan to keep myself sane was regularly checking in with a few fellow outdoor writers I worked with. Along with five or six others, Chris Townsend was one of the people who had been receiving my daily check-in pings from the satellite communicator. I'd been sending texts to these folk when I could too, and their perspectives helped to ground me. People like Chris knew exactly what I was going through.

Chris Townsend is probably the UK's most experienced long-distance backpacker, and bit of a legend in hiking circles. In addition to being the first person to complete a continuous round of all Scotland's Munros and Tops on foot, he was also the first to walk the length of the

Canadian Rockies (1,600 miles), and he hiked the Pacific Crest Trail (2,650 miles) from Mexico to Canada in 1981, well before the trail became the popular objective it is today. He's regarded as an authority on outdoor gear and has been Gear Editor of *The Great Outdoors (TGO)* magazine for many years.

We first met in 2014 when I attended the awards evening for The Great Outdoors Awards. Since then we'd met up several times, and started to work together in 2017 when I took on the role of Online Editor at *TGO*. I'd always admired Chris's passion for long-distance walking, his zeal for defending wild places, and the attitude he'd applied to his life and work. Whenever I found myself overcomplicating things – which was often – I'd usually find that a word or two of advice from Chris would be enough to set me right.

The prospect of Chris joining me for a section of my Cape Wrath Trail was something to look forward to. I wondered how it would colour the experience. Would it be a focal point or a distraction? An encounter that clarified my swirling thoughts about isolation, solitude and connectivity, or one that muddied the waters?

***

Every long-distance trail has a phase I call the hatezone.

The hatezone is a spiral of negativity. Sometimes it's triggered by external circumstances – blisters, hunger, the weather – but not always. It's the dark side of walking alone. It's what sometimes happens when there's nobody else around to cheer you up or offer some perspective. The hatezone can be dangerous. If it spirals too deep, it risks spinning you off trail and into the quitzone.

The less said about the quitzone the better.

On my winter Cape Wrath Trail, the hatezone came for me at about two o'clock in the afternoon on 17 February.

I left Shiel Bridge at about quarter past nine and it was drizzling and mild as I made good time along the road to Morvich. I knew I had a lot of miles to hike through wild and remote country, so I set a steady pace on the easy first section. I met a couple out walking not far from Morvich: him with a silver rucksack cover, peering at a map in its waterproof case; her with purple walking boots and a sunny smile.

The bloke nodded at me. 'Is this the way to the Falls of Glomach? We've heard it's a good walk.'

'Yes, this is the turn-off. There's a bit of climbing, but the path is good.' I squinted at the sky. 'Hope the rain holds off.'

The man nodded. His gaze seemed fixed at the top of my pack, which towered several inches above my head.

'That's a big pack,' the woman said, as if daring to put into words what her partner would not.

'Tell me about it.'

They followed me at a distance, and I last saw them high on the path cutting up and across the hillside above the forest. The rain steadily increased from fine drizzle to heavy rain, then to a continuous downpour. My thin waterproof jacket, a summer model I'd selected for its light weight, soon felt damp and cold inside – a sure sign that the fabric was marinating me in my own condensation. Although I had my gloves and hat on, and was hauling a monstrous pack newly weighed down by fresh supplies up a big hill, I soon began to feel chilly. All around, water poured from the overflowing hillside, spurting from tussocks of grass and flowing back down along the path in a brown gurgle. The mountain's living water was having a party today.

Soon I reached the highest point and began to cross the low plateau before the drop down to the Falls of Glomach. This waterfall, one of the wonders of the West Highlands, is a popular waypoint on the trail and I'd been looking forward to seeing it again. But the path descending the waterfall's gorge could be treacherous at the best of times, and it would require twice as much care today with so much water everywhere. I shivered as I powered ahead through the cold mist. The thought crossed my mind that I should probably stop and put my fleece on, but I didn't want to take off my waterproof and get even more wet than I was already. Stubbornly, I continued, placing my faith in generated body heat.

As I approached the waterfall, I could feel its imprint on my mind long before I could see it – an irresistible force communicated through the bass roar coming up through the ground. No, not the ground, but the water held within this vast sponge over which I roamed. Not a landscape but a hydroscape. Water speaking to water. For a disorienting instant, as I stood there shaking from the cold and the sleet slapping against my cheek, I felt that I understood the connectedness of sky, waterfall, burn and bog. Without the water – the relentless water we hikers curse and swear at for stealing our views and making our lives miserable – this place would be dead and dust. So I listened to the waterfall's weird chant, and the moment passed, and it was once more just white noise on the wind.

I began to drop down into the great zigzag canyon of Allt a' Ghlo-maich, the torrent coming down from the waterfall itself. That roar was thunderous now, the ground palpably shaking as I slithered down the muddy path to the perch high above the gorge where the waterfall could be viewed up close. A slip on one of those rock steps had me wondering if I should have taken off my pack before coming down here. I grabbed handfuls of heather, rowan stalks, clumps of grass to keep me steady. This was no graded scramble, but the rain and the greasy rock and the boom-ing chasm below made me feel suddenly exposed.

Spray filled the chute of rock funnelling the river from the open moor-land into the canyon far beneath. Back at the hotel that morning, the CWT guidebook had informed me that the Falls of Glomach had a maximum fall height of 113 metres. It looked like more. I tried to keep a single mote of water in view as it leapt from the top and plunged to the bottom, only to fail and try again, mesmerised by the swirling galaxies held in constant motion in that column of water.

As soon as I turned away from the waterfall, I felt the cold once again, felt the clammy dampness of my saturated jacket, realised that I could hardly feel my hands as the sleety rain beat down on me. I should have put my fleece on an hour ago, and now I felt more reluctant than ever to stop in this sluicing downpour and get the contents of my pack (and my clothes) even more soaked.

So I kept going, feeling colder and more miserable than ever now that I no longer had the focal point of the waterfall to look forward to.

Top left: Ian Roddie on board *Yorrel* in the 1970s.

Top right: *Yorrel* on the River Deben in the 1970s.

Above: 6 February – Ardnamurchan Point at the start of my journey.

Above: A wild camp at Sanna Bay with my original tent, after its condensation problem had started to make itself felt.

Below: Corryhully bothy on the edge of Knoydart.

Above: A pitstop in a B&B at Salen on 8 February.

Right: Near the summit of Sgùrr nan Coireachan.

Below: Entering Knoydart.
© *James Roddie.*

Top: Bothy life at A'Chuil. © *James Roddie*.

Above left: The Watcher of Sourlies.

Above right: Knoydart's winter glow.

Top left: The regenerating pinewoods of Coille na Glas-Leitire.

Top right: Chris Townsend crossing a river on the section behind Beinn Eighe.

Above: A wild camp with Chris Townsend in a stunning location.

Top: Lochan Fada, on the long stomp between Kinlochewe and Dundonnell.

Above: A wild camp on the edge of Assynt, just after saying farewell to my friend Skye.

Above: The whale skull on the farthest shore at Sandwood Bay.

Below: The uncompromising landscape of Cape Wrath.

Top: 2 March – approaching the lighthouse at Cape Wrath.

Above: The lighthouse beam cutting through the glow of the Milky Way at Kearvaig bothy on the last night.

The steep-sided canyon, while beautiful and undoubtedly of ecological significance due to the vegetated cliffs where deer could not reach, failed to move me as I slipped and slithered down the awkward path, cursing the rocky steps, until I reached a stream crossing where the water came over my gaiters and filled up my waterproof socks. I'd rapidly got to the point in the hatezone spiral where I barely noticed my surroundings and just stomped along the trail in my own little vortex of misery.

By the time the trail spat me out of the gorge, in upper Glen Elchaig, I'd had enough for the day. A gale howled up the glen, slamming blasts of rain against me, forcing me to brace into my poles with every gust.

Part of me wanted to stop and camp, and part of me couldn't stand the idea. There were still eleven kilometres to go to the bothy at Maol Bhuid-he. To my hiker brain, the reasons *not* to stop were unassailable: it wasn't even two o'clock in the afternoon yet, I'd only done fifteen kilometres for the day, and if I stopped now it would throw my plans out of joint. The more rational part of my mind argued that I was tired and cold, and asked me what the hell I was trying to prove anyway – and to whom? My hiker brain won the argument. I kept slogging along the trail and deeper into the hatezone as wave after wave of rain swept across the loch, veiling the hills in the distance. By this point I was so soaked that I doubted even my double line of defence against water would keep any of my gear dry.

***

As it usually does, the hatezone burnt itself out after a couple more hours. Rain showers and sunshine followed me as I powered uphill from Iron Lodge into the vast area of mountain land marked Killilan Forest on the map. Warmth returned to my limbs. I told myself off for flirting with hypothermia.

The bealach between Faochaig and Aonach Buidhe marked another of those boundaries that punctuated my Cape Wrath Trail experience. Beyond, the land felt significantly more wild, more vital, a place of vague paths and greater distances. The light opened up as I traversed this water-scape. Golden-hour spotlights danced on distant hillsides, and snowbeds blinked and flared before fading again beneath a cloud base that didn't quite know what to do with itself. I watched the young threads of torrents clasped so hopefully to every furrow and crease of the mountains, carrying out their unconscious work. Each had a name. Some of those names were marked on the map; others had been forgotten. Their voices were stronger in weather like this, and now that my mood had improved I realised that my day had been all the richer for hearing them.

Maol Bhuidhe: a white geometric fleck amongst the vastness, noticed as something not quite belonging long before I could positively identify it. It drew me on and my pace quickened.

Of course, I had forgotten all about the deep and fast-flowing river crossing right outside the bothy. *What's one more soaking?* I found myself thinking as I waded the flow. My pants were already as wet as they could be.

Inside the bothy, with darkness growing outside, I stripped off, then dangled wet clothing and gear everywhere before changing into my sleeping clothes and down jacket. The bothy windows framed a fading chrome glow that etched shadows and pools of complete blackness in the bothy's interior. I waited for as long as I could before resorting to the head torch, an obliterating moment that blew like a gust through jewelled spiderwebs. My surroundings shifted. The bothy was tamed now. In place of mysterious textures and hidden corners I saw new, smartly varnished woodwork and an information board about the bothy's history.

I looked around for candles, a more sympathetic and less conquering form of light, but found none. What I did find was the bothy book – a slightly damp, curly-paged tome containing the stories of travellers who had spent the night at this remote bastion.

Almost immediately, I found a record that made me punch the air with joy:

16 Feb 19
Walked in with Jon, a great guy also doing CWT. Initially dismayed, no candles, no fuel at all, but found the place very cosy none the less and had a good night sleeping in till 10am. Love the loft, well done to MO [Main-

tenance Officer] and co for such an awesome one. Top marks and bless you all!

Off to do the sketchy river crossing now, it rained all night!

Skye McGregor (age 16, solo on CWT winter)

P.S. Hi Alex, how are you going!

Skye! He had made it through Knoydart. Something within me unknotted. I'd been worrying about how this inexperienced and very young backpacker would cope with Knoydart's rivers and the storm just before Shiel Bridge. He was still on the trail, and by the upbeat tone of his entry he was doing well. I checked my watch; he was a day ahead of me.

The idea of someone hiking faster than me nudged at some deeply embedded competitive instinct, but overriding that was a sense of satisfaction that this young man was on track to complete a massive challenge he'd set himself – something that could define his life. I felt delighted for him and good about my own small role in his safe progress, and as I shuffled around the bothy and looked into its corners and crevices I realised that this notification ping from Skye had lifted my entire day. I'd been spiralling down into the hatezone, but a post from Skye in the weird, analogue bothy social media had boosted me all the way back out. I may have cut myself off from the internet but not from human communication. There was a difference.

I spent the rest of the evening trying to dry my socks over my tiny little backpacking stove, and failing abysmally.

***

Day 13: 18 February 2019

The wind picked up as I descended towards Bendronaig Lodge, and that's when I noticed the ugly scars of fresh roads everywhere: evidence of the new hydro schemes in this valley. It stopped me like a physical shock.

Last time I'd walked through here, humanity's thumbprint on the land had been far lighter. There had been Bendronaig Lodge itself – a couple of white buildings used by the estate, one of which was open as a bothy to walkers – and a quiet little track suitable for four-by-four vehicles, and that was about it. But in 2016 work began on three new run-of-river hydro schemes in the Attadale Estate, and to get the big machinery in to move earth and set concrete they needed roads. *Big* roads.

I stepped from yielding bog on to a moonlike surface of crushed aggregate. The verges looked pulverised, wounded – a piling-up of rocks wrenched from within the land, then a crude ditch with a trickle of black water in the bottom, then the torn edge of heather and moss and grass. To my eye, coming out of that wild and quiet place into this chaos, the road looked as wide as a motorway. A place for roadkill.

Most planning applications for hydro tracks stipulate that the access roads will be restored to a semblance of their former condition after work is completed, but this doesn't always happen. Sometimes the damage is permanent. Sometimes any last remnant of wildness is banished and never comes back.

Wildness in Scotland is a divisive and politicised subject. Some say that landscape is a resource to be exploited – an attitude that has led to the hollowing-out of biodiversity, a flatlining, a silencing. In the nineteenth century, estate keepers would shoot everything that moved.[1] Attitudes change, but in some respects they remain the same. As the self-willed spark drains inch by inch, the land presents itself as more sterile, more bland, less surprising to every generation that follows. We become accustomed to the lack of trees and the silence. What we perceive as normal morphs with surprising speed, a phenomenon known as shifting baseline syndrome – such a bleak concept that a person's life is saddened just by being aware of it. In 1837 there were hundreds of wildcats to be shot in Glengarry. Now the species is close to extinction in the wild.

What does this have to do with access roads for hydro works? Everything. Some argue that protecting wild land is no use because there is no

---

1 On the Glengarry Estate, between 1837 and 1840 alone, gamekeepers slaughtered 27 white-tailed eagles, 15 golden eagles, 18 ospreys, 275 red kites, 198 wildcats, 246 'marten cats' (pine martens), 48 otters, 63 goshawks, 462 kestrels, 285 buzzards and 63 hen harriers. It's thought that this litany of death, while shocking today, was by no means atypical. All wild creatures that could not directly be profited from were considered vermin.

wilderness left, but that's no excuse to do more damage. Nothing is untouched. This doesn't mean we should give up and turn the entire planet into a factory. Wild creatures and natural processes have intrinsic value that have nothing to do with human beings or their motives. It is not just about one little road in the middle of nowhere; it is about our entire attitude towards the great and wonderful sphere of non-human life.

I thought about Chris Townsend again. When we met, our conversations inevitably turned towards wildness, conservation and rewilding. Chris had been a writer and campaigner on these subjects since before I was born, and his work with the John Muir Trust had helped to hold back the tide of development elsewhere, protecting precious wildlife refugia. I wasn't looking forward to telling him about what I'd seen here in the Attadale Estate.

I was soon past the devastation and on to more sympathetic paths, and I navigated Bealach Bhearnais with GPS in hand, fighting against the wind, glad of the fleece I'd had the common sense to layer under my jacket this time. The rain was torrential. For most of the descent I splashed up to my ankles through the water that flowed everywhere, breaking free of burns and channels as the mountain's sponge burst past saturation point. The mountains, from what little I could see of them, were starting to look a little more Torridonian – sheer and terraced with rocky layers climbing high into the clouds. The only snow I could see consisted of isolated patches and a pale dusting of fresher snow above 900 metres on Sgùrr a' Chaorachain. The wind and the wet made it feel cold, but it certainly didn't feel wintry.

After a long descent and a single-wire bridge that looked so terrifying I decided to wade the river instead, I found myself walking through a ghost forest. Peat hags to the side of the track revealed the stumps and roots of huge bog pines, gnarled and twisted as they emerged from the saturated peat, alive with mosses and lichens but otherwise very much dead. Thousands of years ago, trees had grown densely here. I hadn't seen a living tree for hours. There would have been birdsong, and the pawprint of a wildcat in a glade heavy with the pungent aroma of pine needles, maybe a beaver dam down by the river – the tangle and fight and constant surprise of life, not this simplified place of echoes. There was much to love and be thankful for in this landscape, but there was also much to mourn.

Looking across the river, I saw a herd of bedraggled and pinched-looking deer, a dozen or more in all, staring at me across the bare land.

***

Depending on your point of view, Gerry's Hostel in Craig is either the best place in the world or one of the strangest. As I walked down the drive from the main road I thought that the building looked a bit like a converted church, low and neat and whitewashed, although I later learnt that it is in fact two old railway cottages joined together. All of the doors were locked; I hammered on first one and then the others until, after a long time, the hostel manager appeared.

Simon was a tall, thin man in early middle age wearing a frayed woolly jumper and a surprised expression, as if I were the first person he'd seen in several days. When he spoke, his tone was firm but not unfriendly.

'Take your boots off. And your waterproofs too. Can't be having wet things in the hostel.'

I was soaked, as usual. Fair enough.

'Have you received a supply box addressed to me? Name's Alex Roddie.'

'The drying room's through here.' My question hadn't registered.

He shepherded me into the drying room, which was smaller than I expected and mostly seemed to consist of hot pipes and coat hangers.

'It's very important to keep all the wet things in the drying room,' he added, then, 'Roddie, was it? I think there's a box about somewhere. I'll leave it on the stairs.'

I'd heard a lot about Gerry's Hostel, of course. All CWT hikers had. The hostel at Craig is on the Bealach Bhearnais and Coulin Pass variant of the trail; back in 2015 I'd gone further west, but this time I needed somewhere to send a resupply box and this looked like a good opportunity. Gerry's Hostel is the oldest independent hostel in Scotland, established in 1968 by Gerry Howkins, and after Gerry's death in 2015 his son

Simon had taken it on. Gerry had been regarded as a legend in the hiking community. As far as I'd heard, people were still making up their minds as to whether Simon also qualified as a legend, but the hostel itself had changed little for decades.

As I hauled first my rucksack and then my resupply box into the freezing dorm area – I was clearly the only visitor and the heating was off – Simon hovered anxiously nearby.

'I'll put the heating on later if it gets chilly,' he said. 'Should be all right for now. The lounge is through there. Mind you don't put your feet up on the sofa. I'll show you to the kitchen now.'

I dropped my stuff at the bunk closest to a radiator and followed him through a doorway into the lounge. Ancient bookshelves overflowed with decades' worth of outdoor magazines. I saw a well-read copy of *The Great Outdoors* from 1991 poking out from one end of the shelf, and Simon absent-mindedly shoved it back into its place as we walked past. There was a blackened log-burning stove with a huge pile of logs next to it. Simon said he might consider lighting it later on if it got cold enough. The temperature in the lounge was probably only about two degrees higher than it had been outside.

To my delight, I saw a record player next to a towering stack of old classical records. Simon rested his hands on the player.

'Now then, there are important kitchen rules to be aware of … '

After I'd been shown around the small time-warp kitchen and quizzed to make sure I understood the rules, Simon remarked that there would be one more resident staying later on, wished me a good night, and then left me to it. I wandered back through to the lounge, ran my hand over the polished wood of the old table, smiled at the mismatched rugs and faded sofa coverings. There were old maps Blu-Tacked to the walls and a lot of postcards and old photos, some of which seemed to be decades old. This place reminded me of the Clachaig Inn – an unpretentious, old-fashioned, worn-in sort of hospitality. Places like this were being modernised out of existence all the time.

I looked up. The shade for the main ceiling light above me was made from the drum of an old washing machine.

***

Later, after I'd wolfed down one of the dehydrated meal packets from my supply box along with a surplus malt loaf and some chocolate, I sat at the table in the lounge writing up my journal. I'd figured out how to operate the record player and had put on Rachmaninov's Third Piano Concerto, a piece I loved. The rich tones of the vinyl seemed at home in this place of soft edges.

There was some clattering from elsewhere in the building, and soon enough I heard footsteps in the dorm next door, then a voice: 'Thanks, Simon – any chance of the fire on?'

There was a grumble, but after a moment I heard a murmur of assent and Simon came through. He glanced at me on his way to the stove. 'You've got company,' he said.

The newcomer came in and shook my hand before sitting down opposite me at the table. An athletic-looking man with short-cut grey hair, in late middle age, he was clad up and down in vintage Páramo hill clothing and had the look of a veteran hillwalker about him. As we chatted, I heard the smack and split of Simon chopping kindling in the far corner of the room.

'Been up on Chaorachain today,' the walker said with a tired smile. 'Not much snow. I've never seen it so bad in February.'

I soon learnt that his name was Derek. He was sixty-four years old and worked at Sellafield nuclear power station in Cumbria. This was his second combined round of the Munros and Corbetts.

'Some people just do Munros, but I like the quieter hills too, and some of the best are Corbetts, don't you think?' he said. 'On days like this I wonder why I still bother, though. I've been up here a week and haven't seen a view yet. A whole lot of driving and sinking into bogs that should be frozen.' His smile returned. 'Are you Munro-bagging?'

From the stove's corner of the room I heard the crackle and pop of dry kindling catching light, and soon a wavering orange glow stole over the lounge. It seemed to fit with the music of piano and orchestra.

'Backpacking,' I said, and when I outlined what I was up to a wistful expression stole into his eye.

'I hiked the Cape Wrath Trail in 1999 with my late wife,' he said. 'Early March. Added a few of the Tops along the way. Ice axe and crampons over Beinn Eighe – really quite wonderful.'

'Have you seen a recent weather forecast, by the way?'

'Low-pressure zones lined up one after the other out in the Atlantic for the foreseeable. Wind and rain, basically, and freezing levels well above the summits.'

That was more or less expected. I felt a blend of disappointment and relief. This would not be the winter Cape Wrath Trail I had dreamt about. Either my luck was atrocious or this was just the new normal.

'Do you think the best days of Scottish winter are all in the past now?' I asked Derek. 'Do you think winters are going to be brown and wet in future?'

He shrugged. 'I really don't know. It would be a shame, but maybe something so good can't last. Maybe Scottish winter mountaineering was a gift only to a few generations.'

I allowed myself to let go of the dream of a true winter Cape Wrath Trail. I'd visualised days of travel over a silent snowy landscape, stars and aurora burning down at night while I entranced myself with sastrugi by day. It wasn't going to happen. Like the simplification of wildness to something blander and safer, my own journey had become diminished – a summer trail with worse weather than average rather than a different experience altogether. I would embrace and enjoy it for what it was, because life is short and one day I would look back on plodding along a hill track in the mist and rain with unbearable longing. An experience simplified is still an experience, and I had the best parts of the Cape Wrath Trail ahead of me.

Chapter 8

Day 14: 19 February 2019

I received a text from Chris that morning as I left the hostel: 'If you'll be in Torridon today, I'll try to catch you up. Forecast looks foul.'

I sent a reply telling him that I was on the approach to Coire Lair, but didn't receive an answer, and soon I was back up into the hills and out of phone signal again.

With several route options in this part of the trail, I decided to hike up Coire Lair to rejoin my 2015 route beneath Coire Grannda before descending to Glen Torridon. This is big, fine country. The mountains I'd be walking beneath had names like Beinn Liath Mhòr, Sgòrr Ruadh, Fuar Tholl – names that sounded both poetic and warlike to me. I was looking forward to the walk up through Coire Lair. I'd never been there before, and the lower valley had a reputation for quality forest, with some huge surviving granny pines.

Unfortunately I saw little of it as I slogged uphill in the pouring rain. Massive pine trees loomed out of the mist – sentinels, perhaps, or vanguards of a changing landscape, forms both skeletal and sculptural. Soon I was up into the flat expanse of the corrie itself. Although the ascent had been disturbingly muggy, I put my fleece back on for the walk past the loch and up to the bealach. And I kept slowing down, wondering if Chris might be hard on my heels.

At the bealach I met two other walkers coming down from Sgòrr Ruadh – glum-looking men dressed in saturated waterproof clothing, tramping slowly downwards through the murk. I noticed ice axes strapped to their packs, rubber pick guards still in place.

'Aye, we've picked the weather, right enough,' one said to me, wistfully. 'We booked this holiday six months ago. Not a bit of snow up there.'

I descended towards Glen Torridon, getting the camera out a couple of times for dramatic misty views of Beinn Eighe and Liathach. My camera was still working – just. Its focus-mode selector switch had packed in back at Glenfinnan, and there was a little fogging inside the lens, probably because I could never stop it from getting soaked at regular intervals (and no weather-sealed camera is completely waterproof). Despite the drab, overcast conditions, the mountain wall in front of me glowed with colour: a delicate furze of reds, oranges and yellows drybrushed over the horizontally stratified skeleton of rock and scree, while above, on the highest crests, I saw the lightest possible tracery of fresh snow. Soft rain diffused the scene, bringing out the glow in those Velvia colours.

When I reached the little single-track road winding through the bottom of the glen, I asked myself what to do. There was still no sign of Chris. He might be behind, or he might be ahead, but I was already starting to think I wanted to take a day off tomorrow in Torridon village anyway, so I started walking west along the road, breaking away from the line of the CWT for the first time since Glenfinnan.

In less than five minutes, a car pulled over, and I looked through the wound-down window to see Chris Townsend's grinning bearded face and mane of unruly grey hair looking back at me.

'Alex! I've found you, then. How's the walk going?'

***

'How about I drive your pack down to the campsite and you walk along the road? Would that be acceptable, do you think?'

I was glad that Chris suggested this. Even though the walk to Torridon village was off trail, I'm just enough of a purist to be uncomfortable with the idea of hitching a lift. My incredibly heavy pack, however, had been digging in to my shoulders all day and I was only too happy to let it take a ride in Chris's car. As he drove off, I resumed my walk, and without twenty kilos of gear and food dragging me down it felt like I'd suddenly strapped on rocket boots. I floated on air all the way to Torridon.

The campsite was a partially flooded and lumpy field that looked more like a car park. On the plus side, it was free to camp there. I found Chris parked over to one side and stalking to and fro, peering at the ground – or at least what ground could be seen between the enormous puddles – trying to figure out if there were any areas flat enough to take a couple of small backpacking tents. He waved at me as I strolled in. I noticed that his car boot was open, and it was crammed with a pile of outdoor gear: boots, rucksacks, ice axes, crampons, clothing. As Gear Editor for *The Great Outdoors* magazine, Chris always had plenty of new kit to review, and I suspected he'd brought a few items along on this trip to test out.

I dumped my pack on the ground at the far end of the campsite. Chris was moving with an unhurried gentleness, as if he didn't want to disturb the ground over which he walked. He was about seventy, but he had the look of a man who could still carry a heavy pack for days through a rugged mountain landscape. He kept himself fit gear-testing and undertaking ambitious long-distance hikes, such as Yosemite to Death Valley and the GR5 traverse of the Alps. When I am seventy I want to be like Chris.

Then he pointed at the spot he'd selected and said, 'What do you think about that spot? Doesn't look too bad. I'll pitch over here.'

The patch he'd indicated for himself was about ten metres away, and decidedly less flat than the spot he'd proffered to me. I thanked him, and set to work pitching my tent.

*****

It made me smile that, despite the fact that Chris had come over from near Grantown-on-Spey in a car and could therefore bring whatever gear he liked, he'd chosen a lightweight one-person tent – as if he were backpacking himself. As he pitched it, I noticed to my surprise that it was a tent of the same brand as the faulty one I'd sent back with James at Glenfinnan. My sample, which had leaked like a sieve, had been the large, two-person model; this was the smaller one-person version. I'd texted Chris about my tent woes at the time.

He noticed me looking. 'I thought I'd bring it along. I'd tested it before, of course, and the breathable fabric performed fine, but I hadn't really tried it in winter. Based on your report I thought it was worth another go.' Chris ran his hand over the taut green fabric. 'Last time I tried it, it certainly breathed very well.'

'I think mine was just from a bad batch.'

'And how has the rest of your gear performed?'

We geeked out about gear for fifteen minutes or more. I dug the satellite communicator out of my pack's side pocket and complained about its faults: the poky keyboard that was hard to type on, the poor signal, the frustrating software bugs, the subtle way its very presence changed my experience on the trail.

I needed to send a check-in ping anyway, so I demonstrated the procedure to Chris and then waited for the 'sending' message to disappear on the screen. And waited. And waited.

The device was still thinking to itself, so I went over to my tent and propped it up on the ground with the antenna pointing towards the sky. As I did so, I noticed one of my dry bags sitting on the ground in my gear pile. It was the yellow one containing my sleeping bag, and I saw a speck of something dark on the surface – dirt, I assumed at first, but I soon saw it move, and despite the time of year I knew at once what I was looking at.

'It's a tick!' I exclaimed in shock. 'There's a bloody tick on my sleeping bag.'

Chris came over. I picked up the dry bag. There was definitely a tick crawling on it – and not a small one either.

'I don't think I've ever seen a tick this early before,' he said.

Ticks had always been a nuisance for walkers in the Highlands during the summer months, but in recent years they had started to bite earlier and later in the season, and anecdotal evidence suggested that their numbers were increasing. These tiny blood-sucking invertebrates lurk in long grass and heather, waiting for juicy hikers to pass by. Some people pick up dozens on a single walk; others, for reasons poorly understood, are hardly ever bitten. Some ticks carry a nasty infection that can cause Lyme disease. Lyme is bad news. If caught early and treated effectively you might get away with headaches, muscle pain, sickness, fever and exhaustion, but it can lead to complications for years – even death. My brother James had suffered from Lyme disease for much of 2017 and into 2018. Almost two years later, he'd sometimes be affected by mysterious aches and pains that came and went. Cases of tick-borne Lyme disease in Scotland are increasing.[1] Some believe that climate change is to blame.

A tick, on 19 February. What a strange winter.

***

Day 15: 20 February 2019

It rained heavily all night. As I made breakfast the next morning I could hear more rain drumming on my tent's flysheet, and I had the feeling that it wasn't going to let up. After we'd both managed to drag ourselves from the warm, dry cocoons of our tents, Chris welcomed my suggestion of a day off.

There was talk of a short walk later on if the weather improved, but for lunch we gravitated towards the café just down the road in Torridon village. I'd never been to the village before. On my last CWT I hadn't left the trail, and had simply continued around the back of Beinn Eighe towards Kinlochewe, so I was curious to see what kind of a place Torridon was. It soon revealed itself as a cluster of houses strung along a narrow road by the side of the loch, sandwiched between sparse tree cover on the hillsides and the boulders and bladderwrack of the foreshore. There was a seaside smell and a dreary mildness to the air as we strolled along the road to the café, unsuccessfully dodging raindrops. By the time we pushed open the door into the cheerful and surprisingly crowded space

---

1 James, M., Gilbert, L., Forbes, K., Bowman, A., 'Recent Lyme Disease Research in Scotland' (University of Aberdeen), retrieved 21 April 2020, https://macaulay.webarchive.hutton. ac.uk/news/gamefairposters/LucyGilbertposter3.pdf

on the other side our waterproofs were streaming once again.

We ordered coffees and cheese scones and went to sit at a table by the window. Rain pattered against the glass. We chatted about the highs and lows of my hike, about (inevitably) work, about the gear I was carrying. After a few minutes our food and drink arrived.

'So, what has it been like not using the internet since you started?' Chris asked me after a while. 'Has it helped?'

Last time we'd spoken about my experiment I'd been hazy on the details of exactly what I wanted to achieve, because I didn't know myself. I didn't know to what extent my anxiety was being influenced by the internet, or some aspect of my participation in it; this was about finding out. Chris's attitude towards technology and the internet had always struck me as straightforward and practical. He was computer literate and interested in new technologies. Unlike many hikers of his generation, he'd wholeheartedly embraced GPS and digital navigation – to a degree some people found surprising, in fact. He was as active on social media as I was, but he had a significantly larger online following. Overall I'd gained the impression that Chris didn't fully understand my stance, that he hadn't noticed any of the downsides that troubled me. He was a prolific writer and author. If he suffered from fragmented attention and compulsive thinking while maintaining an online presence then it certainly didn't show.

'It's been surprising,' I replied. 'I *have* noticed a change in my thinking. My mind is running clearer, if that makes sense, and that jittery restlessness has gone. I don't know if that's just the chilled feeling from being on the trail, though. Overall it's made less of an impression than I thought it would, and in some respects things have been a lot harder. Keeping up with weather forecasts, trying to deal with mishaps and so on without the internet has been challenging.'

He smiled. 'You won't have had signal much anyway. When I'm on a long walk I only go online every few days. People think I'm on social media more than I actually am, because I write posts that all get uploaded at once when I come into signal. I certainly haven't noticed it detracting from my experience. If I did, then I would have stopped long ago.'

'I sometimes wonder if there's something wrong with people of my generation,' I said. 'The internet wasn't around when we were young kids, but suddenly in the late nineties it was everywhere, just when we were entering our teens. That's got to leave a mark. Some damage, perhaps.'

'Perhaps,' Chris said, although he didn't sound convinced. 'Thinking back to many of my long walks, I didn't even have a phone. It was just how things were. I never found the solitude overbearing, but I don't miss the lack of connection either. Being able to connect with people at home, share photos from the trail, is something I really appreciate. I've always been happy being by myself for weeks at a time, though.' He smiled again. 'I can see how constantly being online would detract from the experience. Even if I have signal, I tend to just keep my phone in airplane mode and only go online occasionally.'

'So do I, but it bothers me that I can pull my phone out of my pocket and – bam! – the whole web streams into my head. There's always that feeling not far away, that impulse to just check something. Do you see what I mean? True solitude is denied on a basic level even if you want it.' I remembered Knoydart, and suddenly I felt on uncertain ground. 'That's what I believed at the start of this walk, anyway. I'm not so sure now.'

***

It was still raining, but we couldn't stay in the café forever, so we decided to go for a walk. Chris suggested the hike known as the Woodland Trail from Kinlochewe up through the Beinn Eighe National Nature Reserve to the Conservation Cairn.

There was a gleam of excitement in my companion's eyes as we got ready in the car park at the base of the climb. 'It's been nearly twenty years since I last did this walk,' Chris told me when we set off beneath the silent trees. 'I'm looking forward to seeing how the regeneration has progressed.'

The trail climbed immediately into exquisite forest, dense and watchful. I felt as if we were walking along a corridor held tightly between friezes of heather, blaeberry and rowan scrub, with walls of pine boughs overarching us – a fractal textured world of infinite complexity and beauty. As rain dripped from above and I looked through windows in the canopy to see shreds of mist ghosting over the rocky knuckles of the heights, something deeply embedded within me whispered that this was a place of significance. Of value beyond human calculation. I knew something about the background to this nature reserve already, but that did not invalidate this primal, fluttering instinct that said *magic dwells here.*

The Beinn Eighe National Nature Reserve was established in 1951 – the UK's first NNR – in order to protect the largest surviving fragments of ancient Caledonian pine forest, the woods of Coille na Glas-Leitire. The nature reserve includes much open moorland as well, and, since 2014, the islands of Loch Maree, but the site's true value lies in the quality of its woodland. In the 1950s and 1960s, conservationists began an experiment in woodland regeneration here, excluding grazing deer and planting hundreds of trees. More recently, activity has shifted to thinning the established tree cover, providing deadwood for a range of species. Tree planting is ongoing, but much regeneration is now happening naturally. It's one of the UK's finest examples of successful rewilding. Coille na Glas-Leitire is now a precious habitat for creatures such as the wildcat, golden eagle and pine marten.

'When you talk to people about rewilding,' Chris said to me as we walked up through flourishing woodland in an area that had been bare, degraded hillside decades before, 'sometimes they think it's all about bringing back bears and wolves, and they get defensive. But it's more than that. It's about restoring habitats and ecosystems that we've damaged, giving nature a helping hand to recover.'

Soon we moved out of the dense woodland and on to rugged, more sparsely wooded slopes. The wind drove rain into our faces now, knocking us about on the increasingly exposed path, and this little stroll started to feel a bit more like a hill day. As we struggled against the wind, Chris spoke about the background and history of this incredible place – how techniques pioneered here helped to inform and inspire a wave of rewilding programmes throughout the Highlands. Gradually, thanks to patient conservation work, Scotland's ancient pinewoods were starting to recover in a few sites. It was slow work, but Chris had already witnessed a remarkable transformation.

'I first visited Beinn Eighe on my Land's End to John o'Groats walk, back in 1978,' he told me. 'Walking through, like you are now. It looked very different then. The expansion in tree cover is incredible.'

We reached the Conservation Cairn – a pile of rocks in an exposed location at about 550 metres on the flank of Meall a' Ghiubhais. In good weather, I'd been told, the views from here were magnificent. Dense clouds blasted over the mountains and a sting of rain kept us turned from the wind. I could see very little ahead; behind, we looked down on the green canopy of the forest, with Loch Maree and the brooding wall of Slioch far beyond. It was a truly wild panorama with a natural treeline. Few places in Scotland could boast a view like that. It reinforced what I'd been subconsciously missing elsewhere on my journey: this perfect melding of woodland and mountain, water and sky, life and growth.

'It's wonderful to see how the forest has grown back,' Chris said to me, holding his hood in place against the torrential rain as he looked down on the forest. 'I wonder what it'll look like in another twenty years. I think there are a lot of threats to wild land on the horizon, sadly.'

In his slightly wistful smile I thought I saw the recognition that in another two decades he might not be here to see how this place had thrived, or failed, but that I might be. The weight of that responsibility struck me all at once.

Chris spoke little of his own efforts as a champion for conservation and rewilding, but I knew that he'd played a significant role. He was a trustee of the John Muir Trust (and a member since 1997), the conservation charity dedicated to defending wild land. He had an admirable track record in environmental campaigning too.

'I think this is one of the most hopeful places in all of Britain,' Chris said to me. 'It really puts everything else into perspective.'

It certainly did. As we turned away from the gale and descended back into the woods, I realised that thoughts of my own anxiety, and various hang-ups about the internet, had never been further from my mind.

PART 4

Immanence

Chapter 9

Day 16: 21 February 2019

There are several contenders for the best stage of the Cape Wrath Trail, but few would deny that the rough and beautiful leg around the back of Beinn Eighe is in the top five. My memories of this section from my 2015 CWT were that it felt like a turning point – a point beyond which time slowed and my perspective permanently changed. Mountains are mirrors. We project our experiences on to them, and they reflect our own souls back. Torridon, however, felt more like a prism to me, refracting the light of experience.

Chris and I left Torridon campsite later than I'd planned. This was something I had learnt about him: he doesn't do early mornings. The previous evening, when I'd said 'Shall we make a start at 9.30 tomorrow?' he'd replied 'Getting up or getting going?' I meant getting going, but in the end we didn't even leave the campsite until at least 10.30. I wanted to see if I could get all the way to Kinlochewe that day. Temperatures were rising, and the tidal forces of spring were acting on my hiker brain to make me crave bigger miles and wider horizons again. I could no more resist it than can the swallow or the chiffchaff. Caught in a metamorphosis between slow-and-steady winter mountaineer and fast-and-light summer hiker, I felt an odd buzzing tension that morning as I rattled around the campsite packing my portable home back into my rucksack and waiting for Chris to strike camp.

We started our day's walk at the base of Coire MhicNobaill, the long glen coming down out of the heart of Torridon. This was a big extension on the 'official' line of the CWT, which resumed a long way to the east, but I was curious to explore the western part of this area and see a few new places I'd never been. The plan was for us to walk together for the day. Chris had to be back home near Grantown-on-Spey at some point tomorrow, but was otherwise in no hurry; he'd brought his backpacking gear, and was eager to spend a night on the hill. As the clock crept towards eleven o'clock it dawned on me that I would not make it as far as Kinlochewe that day. Any frustration I felt at this dissipated as I realised that we'd probably get to camp somewhere north of Beinn Eighe. Besides, what really was the hurry?

A slaty grey slab of cloud hid all of the mountains from view as we began our walk. Invisible somewhere to the left was Beinn Alligin and its famous pinnacles, but as we slowly walked uphill beside a gorge lined with birches and alive with the dance of water we could have been almost anywhere in the Highlands.

As the path climbed, we soon left the edges of the gorge and broke out on to the open slopes. Waterfalls laden with rain crashed down over cataracts in the river. We squinted up into the mist but could make out little beyond one tiny snow patch, strikingly isolated hundreds of metres above – the only snow we could see in any direction. I'd been looking forward to seeing the famous view up into the north corries of Liathach, a wild place of hidden lochans and black crags, but we could see nothing at all, not even the slightest hint of a mountain in that direction. The hammer of cloud had come down and could not be resisted. It was a curious flattening of place into somewhere that felt quieter, less special, exhausted somehow, the mountains' voices muffled. Magic snuffed.

'Quite amazingly free of snow for the time of year,' Chris said. 'It feels more like a day in October.'

I too had been getting an October vibe – or perhaps the dregs of April, after that final flash of winter splendour but before spring's green tendrils reach this northern place and bring a different kind of magic. Different seasons have distinct feelings to them. This certainly did not feel like February. Or perhaps it was a new kind of February.

After a few kilometres we joined the main line of the CWT heading up to Coire Mhic Fhearchair. It was raining by this point, a dull stippling of rain that broke up the mirrors of the lochans, but the air felt close and still and so mild that I was overheating in my waterproof overtrousers. Chris hadn't even bothered to change into his waterproofs and was quite happily walking in his windproof top, unfazed by the dampness. We met several other walkers coming down the good path from the upper corrie, but unfortunately when we got there the famous Triple Buttresses of Beinn Eighe were completely hidden by the cloud – just like last time I'd been here, on my 2015 hike.

I felt a little cheated. Coire Mhic Fhearchair is one of the most beautiful places in Scotland. I knew the folklore of the Lancaster Bomber crash, the twisted wreckage lodged in Fuselage Gully that climbers used as a belay anchor to this day. I'd seen the awe-inspiring landscape photography of a graceful multi-tiered crag split by gullies rising above the crystal waters of the loch. I'd even admired paintings of great beauty inspired by this place. But I'd never seen it for myself, because every time I came here the visibility was so poor I could barely see the loch, let alone the mountain.

From this point our route left paths behind and struck out across open country. The character of our day changed at once as we picked our way with care across the torrent surging out of the loch. It was to be the first of several minor river crossings, proof of the fact that we had stepped off the path and into truly wild country. The goal for this next stage, according to my Cicerone guide, was to stick to roughly the 400-metre contour as the Cape Wrath Trail (invisible on the ground, more concept than trail at this point) wandered eastwards around the northern flank of Beinn Eighe's many protruding peaks and valleys. This mountain is a complete massif, not an individual peak, and that's nowhere more obvious than from this vast open space of rock and heather and bog between Beinn Eighe and Glen Grudie.

As we picked our way over the rough ground, Chris and I talked – about outdoor gear, especially the history of firms Chris had dealt with over the years, and the development of trail shoes and waterproof/ breathable fabrics. After a while, the conversation veered back towards my investigation into the outdoors, the internet and anxiety. Drizzle continued to spatter as we picked our way through the heather and around the rocks, making slow progress and gradually dropping beneath the 400-metre contour into boggier but less steep ground below.

'I think I started this trip with preconceived ideas,' I told Chris after a while. 'I had it all figured out. I was going to learn that removing myself from the internet was the one thing I needed to do to solve my anxiety. It hasn't worked out like that.'

'Mental health can be complex,' Chris said, or more shouted to me as he hopped over a stream. 'And sometimes with anything in life it can be the hidden factors we never even consider that have the greatest impact.'

Hidden factors. Things that, perhaps, had always been there but I hadn't wanted to acknowledge.

'I'm also in two minds about the relationship between the outdoors and anxiety,' I said. 'There seems to be this idea – a trendy idea, even – that spending time outside is a panacea for improving mental health and banishing anxiety. I'm not so sure. I mean, at the start of my walk I was stressing myself silly worrying about resupply parcels and gear failures, and I found myself thinking that outdoor adventure can be just as stressful as everyday life. Especially if you don't have internet access to smooth over these problems. What do you think?'

'It's a message that brands like to promote,' Chris said. 'Magazines too, and bloggers. Like many social-media-friendly ideas it can be portrayed in an overly simplistic way at times, though. It's interesting that you found the start of your walk an anxious experience. Similar things have happened to me, but things usually settle down after a week or two, after I get into my flow.'

I found myself nodding. I was into my flow now. After Knoydart everything had felt very different.

'In some circumstances I think that pushing the idea of the outdoors being a cure-all for mental health problems can be dangerous,' I said. 'Take my brother James. He has suffered from clinical depression since he was a teenager. Years ago he started getting into increasingly risky solo rock and ice climbing because it made him feel alive, made him feel like he was achieving something. Outdoor adventure fed into a negative spiral of behaviour that probably would have killed him had he not broken out of it. He's said to me that the outdoors can be both his biggest friend and greatest enemy.'

Chris remained silent, perhaps sensing that I was working through an idea in my head and needed the space to figure it out.

'It's really exposed the oversimplification in that "get outside and everything will be fine" narrative we see online so often,' I continued, 'and it's exposed the bullshit in my own stance about the internet too. It's all so much more complex, more nuanced, than I thought. Spending too much time online probably was having an effect on me. So were other factors.'

'Do you think it's been worthwhile?' Chris asked.

I thought for a moment before replying. 'Learning something new about yourself is always worthwhile, I think.'

***

Although our route around the back of Beinn Eighe was challenging, it wasn't as pathless as I remembered. In 2015, I'd seen no hint of a path anywhere between Loch Coire Mhic Fhearchair and the start of the stalker's path heading to Kinlochewe – a distance of at least six rough, uncompromising kilometres. This time, as we clambered over hillocks and descended into troughs, worked our way around steep sections, avoided scree slopes, and generally went about the time-consuming work of trying to stick to a course over rough ground, we kept coming across faint sections of path. We'd lose these vague tracks almost as quickly as we found them. I'd asked Chris if he thought they were deer tracks, but he thought not, and I wondered out loud if they might be new paths created by backpackers on the Cape Wrath Trail – 'desire lines', imprinted into the ground as everyone found their own way.

'It's possible,' Chris had replied. 'The Cape Wrath Trail has become more popular in the last few years, from what I hear.'

'That's at least a little my fault,' I said. 'I hiked the trail in 2015 then immediately published a whole bunch of magazine articles and blog posts. It must have had an effect. There's more rubbish in bothies now too. I worry about my impact as an outdoor writer sometimes.'

'We do have an impact. That can't be denied, but people who come here grow to love these places, and if nobody loved them then there would be nobody to stand up for them – nobody to protect them.'

I hadn't considered that. 'So you think our impact is a net positive?'

'Put it this way,' Chris said, 'without outdoor writers, it's probable that much more of our wild land would have been exploited by industry by now – ancient forests logged, glens flooded by hydro developments. Look at how the outdoor community comes together in resisting inappropriate wind farm proposals on wild land.'

I looked down at the trail beneath my feet. A fuzzy consensus was being drawn up by hundreds of pairs of boots as the easiest line was gradually worked out and walked on, imperceptibly carved into the earth. This is how trails are born. Part of my soul thought that any diminution of the wildness here was a shame – that a path would forever tame the raw experience of questing through this landscape. But part of me knew that it was inevitable. No route is pathless forever – and yet perhaps in other aeons there had been paths here before, paths obliterated by the glaciers and softened by the peat. On a long enough timescale all paths are reclaimed by nature. That thought comforted me.

Impact, legacy, deep time, the meaning of wildness. Perhaps those were the true questions my mind was working over on this long journey. I wondered what it would conclude before the end.

***

By the time the weather started to clear at about four o'clock, it was obvious that I wouldn't make it to Kinlochewe that day. I didn't mind, though. Glorious light had begun to spread on the hills, and wisps of cloud boiled off the snow patches surviving high on Beinn Eighe. Our miles had been won hard, bartered from the rock and the bogs as we crested moraine ridge after moraine ridge, and I was starting to think about looking for somewhere to camp.

'There's always somewhere,' Chris said. 'It's just a case of finding it.'

I was getting better at finding good camping spots, but it is a subtle art and not easily learnt. Most ground in Scotland is not suitable for pitching a tent on: too lumpy, too wet, too rocky, too heathery. Most of the terrain we'd crossed that day had qualified as all four, but as we descended towards the river that now meandered in lazy loops between the heights of Ruadh-stac Beag (another of Beinn Eighe's quartzite ramparts) and Meall a' Ghiubhais (an attractive terraced hill to the north) we realised that this area would be our best bet. I poked at some tussocky knolls while Chris paced back and forth beside a bend in the river, peering at the ground with that calm, attentive alertness I'd seen in Torridon campsite. Here was a man who knew exactly what to look for in a camping spot, even in a complex place such as this, and was confident of finding it.

I found myself staring into a pool where a standing wave was perpetually breaking over a submerged boulder. The water was as clear as any I'd seen, alive with refracted light from the sky and swaying green fronds below. A thousand pebbles lined the riverbed. Each was a world to itself. Each was a different shape, a different colour, a different maze of textures. I gazed down into the pool, mesmerised, utterly absorbed, and of myself I saw only a rippled shadow reflected back – a dark mass sparking with highlights, identity absorbed by the river. A ghost in a standing wave. Perhaps that's all any of us are.

Hours later, after we'd pitched tents and cooked meals, gas stoves hissing in that vast silence broken only by the endless murmur of the river next to us, I unzipped my tent and crawled out into the darkness. The night air was cold enough for me to put my down jacket and insulated trousers back on. I'd been snug in my sleeping bag, and getting out of a tent always feels like a huge hassle once you're in – I particularly loathe forcing wet boots on to newly dried feet – but I thought I'd been able to sense clear skies above and stars twinkling down, even though I couldn't see them.

I was right. After my eyes adjusted to the darkness, I beheld the haze of stars above, obscured only partly by wisps of high-level cloud. Chris's tent glowed orange with the light of his head torch – he was probably reading in his sleeping bag. I turned my own torch off and felt my self dissolve into the darkness. Now Chris's glowing tent was the only sign of artificial light as far as I could see: a mote of humanity cradled within a place indescribably precious and fragile.

When we left this place, we would leave no trace but the imprints of our tents on the grass. Chris would walk back the way he had come, to his car in Torridon village, while I would walk on. Both of us would later write about this experience. What impact would that writing have on the tangible reality I stood amongst at that moment – the colours on the rocks in the riverbed, the breeze-stirred grasses, and the monumental shadows of the mountains rising as pyramids against a star-filled sky? Was the eternal standing wave in the river truly eternal? Would the river dry up, the heather burn, the shapes those mountains cast in our minds warp and change into different metaphors for a different people in a different time? What place did I have in that immensity?

Words can create landscapes, and they can destroy them too. I thought about Chris's perspective, his optimism, as I stood there under the clear and frostless February sky. Words – my own, maybe – had helped to carve fresh paths through this landscape, paths that would perhaps in time be marked on official maps and bring more people who would drop more litter and create more pollution. But words would also help those same people to love this place and fight for it. Words had safeguarded the precious sanctuary of Coille na Glas-Leitire for decades, and would sway its fate into the distant future. Impact goes both ways. My own words had not yet been written, and neither had their imprint on the natural world.

As I watched the glow from Chris's tent, I thought about how good it had felt to walk with someone else for a change, share ideas, get a fresh perspective. Although happy in my own company, I'd long ago learnt that ideas can spiral in on themselves when I spend too much time by myself, unspooling into imaginary narratives and conversations that tend to point in the direction of anxiety and worry. Perhaps, I realised, that's what happens when I spend too much time online. To be *very online* is to be in a toxic collective solitude where everyone is battling their own demons in their own infinite echo chamber, their own confirmation-bias machine. I felt as if I'd broken free of all that for a while. Solitude is good and valuable in the right proportion, but so is connection. Ideas might grow in silence but they can't thrive without other people.

I'd come on this Cape Wrath Trail looking for ultimate solitude, and yet to my surprise this section walking with someone else had proven to be one of the most worthwhile so far. A time for solitude, and a time for connection.

My days with Chris had felt refreshing, but now I was looking forward to heading off by myself again – looking forward to the final stage of my journey to Cape Wrath.

Chapter 10

Day 17: 22 February 2019

I said goodbye to Chris early the next morning. I'd already woken, had breakfast and begun to pack away my shelter, sodden with dew, by the time I heard signs of life from inside Chris's tent. Soon the telltale roar of a backpacking stove rose above the river's ceaseless gurgle. I looked down into the pool for the standing wave that had mesmerised me the previous evening, but it was invisible now, all definition lost in the flat light from an overcast sky.

By the time I'd packed away my gear and had finished faffing, Chris was up and about. According to his pocket weather station the barometric pressure had risen to 102 millibars overnight. Temperatures had remained well above freezing.

'The high pressure is forecast to continue,' Chris told me. 'I think you'll have some good weather for the next bit.'

I nodded, gazing eastwards towards the bealach. 'Thanks for coming along with me for this section. I've really enjoyed it.'

We shook hands and he waved as I squelched off through the bogs.

Twenty minutes later, I looked behind me and could see Chris's tent still, but only because I knew where to look, and only if I looked hard: a tiny fleck of brighter green in the vastness, dwarfed by the stone-shouldered bastions of Beinn Eighe.

***

To me, the Cape Wrath Trail felt like a journey of thresholds; of approaching, negotiating with and then breaching invisible boundaries. I felt myself nudging the edges of another boundary as I climbed up to the bealach that would lead me beneath the Conservation Cairn and down to Kinlochewe. Behind me, the views could hardly be more impressive. The peaks of Spidean Coire nan Clach and Sgùrr Bàn rose high above the depths of the glen, showing off their purple-grey cloaks of scree, trimmed with the extravagant ermine of those few snow wreaths that had survived the thaw.

I was passing beyond Torridon and into the wild and rugged area known as Fisherfield – a tough section, but I was looking forward to it. Shenavall was the highlight: a legendary bothy nestled at the foot of An Teallach, the serrated mountain range whose name translates to 'the forge' in English.

Shenavall had long held a magnetic allure for hikers and climbers alike. For the first time in a few days, I remembered Skye McGregor, the young LEJOG hiker I'd last heard from in the Maol Bhuidhe bothy book, and wondered if I'd bump into him again on this section. Was he still ahead of me? Had I overtaken him? That hardly seemed likely, as I'd had a day off in Torridon, but there was no way of knowing unless Skye had left a note in the next bothy book. And the next bothy book was at Shenavall.

Now that I was by myself again, I could already feel my life contracting back to the radical simplicity I so loved about being on the trail. Today's mission: to pick up a few supplies at Kinlochewe, and then to see if I could get as far as Shenavall. At around thirty-five kilometres, it was a big day indeed for the time of year, but the spring sap rising in me could not be resisted, and I couldn't help the allure of an ambitious day's target even though part of me wanted to slow down and take the time to enjoy where I was.

The morning wore on and I soon hit the good stalkers' path cresting the bealach and carrying me out of Torridon. Already, Beinn Eighe was 'over there' rather than a landscape I was actively engaging with. The living mountain could become no more than scenery with such swiftness, but I told myself that I wouldn't forget what Beinn Eighe had taught me, wouldn't let it become just another hill. Below and beyond, I felt the village of Kinlochewe drawing me on.

***

As trail towns go, Kinlochewe is just about perfect. It has a hotel with an unpretentious hiker-friendly bunkhouse, a campsite, a pub with a good range of Scottish real ales and a bewildering selection of single-malt whiskies, a hiker-friendly shop at the garage just outside the village, and a general store with anything the hiker could possibly need. I rocked up at the general store and dumped my pack next to the picnic table outside before heading in. Time to satisfy my hiker hunger.

I was the only customer inside the Tardis-like shop, which was all narrow corridors between towering shelves, infinite cans and packets of Pasta 'n' Sauce. The shopkeeper watched me as I trundled up and down the aisles, grabbing items at random and filling my basket to the brim.

At this stage on any long-distance trail I would always be burning more calories than I could stuff into my face. I hated carrying too much food weight and therefore didn't carry it. This under-eating on the trail led to over-eating in town, which more or less balanced itself out (although I often wondered how sustainable this approach would be on a truly long-distance hike over multiple months). I piled my basket high with malt loaf, cereal bars, chocolate, instant coffee, pasta, apples, and anything else I could either eat straight away or cook on my tiny stove.

When I found my way to the till, the shopkeeper nodded and said, 'Cape Wrath Trail hiker, aye?'

I nodded. 'How do you know?'

'I always know,' he said, tapping the side of his nose as he started keying the prices of my items into his till. 'You're the first I've seen in at least a month.'

That surprised me. 'Really? You haven't met a young lad called Skye? Tall, blond hair?'

'No, don't think so.' He paused and rubbed his hands together. 'Great weather, isn't it, now that the rain's gone? You're lucky. It's often awful cold at this time of year. Hopefully we'll get more early tourists like your-self. Maybe with global warming we'll get more Cape Wrathers through-out the year.'

I briefly explained what I was doing as he finished adding up my bill. 'It feels more like May than February,' I added. 'I was hoping for snow travel and snow camping – something that felt more like real winter.'

'You must be mad,' the shopkeeper said. His smile had faded a little. 'The lack of snow has been wonderful this year. Long may it last, I say.'

As I sat at the picnic table outside the shop and proceeded to eat a third of the food I'd bought, I thought about the shopkeeper's perspec-tive. From his point of view as a local business owner, snow was an incon-venience, and bad winter weather was one of the things keeping visitors away from this tiny and relatively isolated place throughout the winter months. Yes, I could understand why our perspectives on winter would be very different. But if winter as we knew it did disappear entirely, if the snows never returned, what greater damage would it cause, what invis-ible cracks would fracture this place?

I checked my phone. There were three bars of signal.

***

'You need to give your mum a ring,' Hannah told me when I rang her. 'She's been ill, although she told me not to tell you.'

Hello again, anxiety.

There seemed to be a connection between my trips to the mountains and family illness. Dad's death had coincided with a plan to go back to Glen Coe. The symptoms of his first bout of cancer had started to bite while I'd been backpacking in the Pyrenees in 2016.

I phoned her. 'Hannah tells me you're ill.'

A slight but telling pause. 'I'm fine. Where are you? How did you get on walking with Chris Townsend? I remember when you had a copy of his *Backpacker's Handbook* when you were a Scout. It's so nice that you work together now.'

I tried to not let her change the subject. 'Is it another abscess?'

'Nothing to worry about, honestly. Just a small infection. I'm on antibiotics. Hannah has been looking after me.'

I tried to read between the lines. My mum had been through a lot in her life. She'd waited years for opportunities to come along, only for them to be cruelly snatched away. She'd suffered tragedies nobody should have to face. This history, some of which even I was not fully aware of, manifested itself in ways that could be difficult to predict. She could be at once fragile and yet also remarkably stoic. She bore the pain of having been strong for too many years, and now she was going through even harder times, struggling to adapt to a new and lonely world without her husband. Fortunately for her, she lived only just round the corner from me and Hannah. This did, however, mean that the pressure fell on Hannah when I was away in the mountains – something I had been keenly aware of before this trip.

'What kind of an infection?'

'Just my tooth again. You know, like last time.'

Last time had been an abscess requiring emergency surgery. Nevertheless, I felt myself relax a little. The fact that she was on antibiotics (rather than, say, in A&E) meant that it probably wasn't that bad after all. Also, it was something *known*. It was not the hurricane of the unknown, the diagnosis out of the blue.

I told her about my adventures, tried to say a few words about the slowness and the simplicity, but something gets lost in translation when you try to bring feelings from the trail across the veil into the Real World. I could tell that she didn't grasp what I was trying to communicate.

'It feels like such a long time since I've seen you,' she said. 'How long before you get to the end?'

'I'm not sure.' I could hear the wariness in my own voice; I didn't really want to think about coming to the end of the trail yet, but I knew that Mum wouldn't see it this way. I forced a change in my tone. 'Perhaps ten days. The weather's improving. It feels more like summer.' I paused. 'Let me know how the infection goes, won't you? Keep me up to date. I want to hear the moment it gets any worse.'

'The thing is, you're out of contact most of the time, aren't you?' She gave a short and awkward laugh. 'I just struggle not seeing you, that's all.

It would be nice to see photos from your trip. I always look forward to your tweets when you're out walking.'

There was no accusation in her voice, just a statement of how she felt. She had accepted the terms of my journey. My terms been hard to accept at first, but accept them she had, as had my wife. Now both were making sacrifices to support me. Hannah was looking after my mum in addition to helping me on the trail and running her own business. Mum was suffering from health problems and depression that, I forced myself to admit, would inevitably be flaring up in part due to my absence. I was causing damage by being here and by intentionally cutting myself off from some forms of contact.

For the first time on my Cape Wrath Trail, I wondered if the indulgence of being offline, of seeking an extra layer of solitude above that already imposed by the trail, might be a luxury I had never really been able to afford. Maintaining the illusion of being adrift from the internet's dazzling distractions was placing an ever-increasing strain on the people I loved. Was my journey a selfish act?

I hung up the phone feeling like a bad son, wondering once more if my journey had failed. As I left Kinlochewe, I gave myself permission to seek bigger miles, to hike longer days. I would reach Cape Wrath and I would get home to the people whose absence I felt more with every passing day.

***

Despite having a damned good go, I didn't make it to Shenavall bothy that day after all. It was a warm and muggy trudge up the track to the Heights of Kinlochewe, a cluster of houses at the end of a gravel track up a secluded glen. Last time I'd been here I'd been delighted by the stands of regenerating woodland growing safe behind deer fences – the core of a new forest. This time the scars of fresh hydro developments dampened my mood. There was no breeze at all, which made the gentle ascent of Gleann na Muice stifling, and after less than a kilometre I unzipped my trouser vents from knee to waist in an attempt to get some airflow. I rolled up my shirtsleeves and shifted the abominable weight of my pack on sore collarbones. The clomping mountaineering boots on my feet felt particularly pointless. A warm, listless sun filtered through cloud above, and I remembered the fact that it was February – a fact that every sense in my body rejected.

As I battled uphill, feeling unfit and whale-like under the weight of all the stuff I was carrying that was so unsuited to the present conditions, I found myself fantasising about my ultralight summer kit. I could ring Hannah when I got to Ullapool and ask her to send up my trail shoes, lighter shelter, down quilt and pack; I could send home the ice axe and crampons, the massive boots, the big pack, the winter sleeping bag, the three kilos of camera gear that for some reason I had decided I had to have, tripod and all. Winter Alex is 'pack all the kit for every eventuality' Alex. These decisions felt like they had been made by a different person now. I wanted a light pack and I was fed up of the discomfort, fed up of the knowledge that I'd optimised my gear so poorly.

The walk improved after the track thinned to an elegant stalkers' path, winding around and over the landscape sympathetically instead of carving right through. Views of the big mountains around Lochan Fada began to open up ahead of me as I left the path all too soon and began a trackless stint uphill towards Bealach na Croise – a section that required careful navigation. Keeping an eye on my GPS, I climbed slowly uphill towards the hidden loch that I knew waited for me just beyond the lip of the hill above. The sun peeked through under the cloud. For a few moments golden light flooded the landscape, turning peat hags and boggy ground into achingly beautiful splendour. Despite the drumbeat of urgency in me now, the drive to reach Cape Wrath, I stopped at the shore of the loch for ten minutes and tried to recapture some of the rapt absorption I'd first experienced in Knoydart.

It took me a few moments to spot the group of red deer hinds huddled against the hillside a few hundred metres away. They were almost precisely the same colour as the rich red-brown grasses that sighed and rippled in the warm breeze. Unless the animals moved, the camouflage illusion was perfect, and my eyes swam as I looked at them, the pattern breaking up in my mind. There they were, and then in the next moment boundary between beast and land had blurred, as if both were part of the same continuum. Above, my gaze wandered to the snow patches and rock scars, scree slopes and forgotten places where humans never bothered to go. *We know nothing, really,* was the only thought that crossed my mind.

I walked on and entered the labyrinth of peat hags. I knew I wouldn't make it to Shenavall now, but I didn't mind.

***

The light failed with shocking speed before I was free of the peat hags, leaving me to make the final climb to Bealach na Croise in growing darkness. A dainty cairn marked the highest point of an otherwise undistinguished heathery saddle where a black stream oozed from pool to pool. I strained to look for the telltale signs of tent-friendly ground, reluctant to get my head torch out and obliterate what night vision I had. There was nowhere to camp here. Onward.

As I made my descent from the bealach I told myself that I wouldn't get out my torch until I had found somewhere to camp. Night fell and my vision shifted from colour to monochrome and the edges of everything began to blur, dancing with false movement like the grainy static of an antique television. The sky, although growing fainter by the moment, looked impossibly bright now as my eyes strained to make out the shreds of a path I was trying to follow downhill. Shades of blue melted into deeper shades one by one.

This is how travellers would have experienced nightfall in these mountains centuries ago, I told myself. *No electric light then.* The knowledge that I had a head torch in my pack allowed this little thrill of danger to feel luxurious. Extravagant, perhaps. I stood there in what was suddenly near-total darkness and allowed myself to feel the emotions that sprang from being alone on a mountain at the failing of the day far from any inhabited place. The stars started to come out, first one and then a dozen or more, and I gazed up at them; they seemed to twinkle more than usual, glowing huge as orbs in the last of the twilight.

Stripped of the tech safety net dormant in my pack, the products engineered to insulate me from almost all possible sources of harm, I would be a small and vulnerable mammal cast adrift in a scary place. The landscape would be alive in a way that I could only dimly imagine. I had the gear necessary to keep me safe. Not everyone who ventures into the Scottish mountains has the full range of specialist and often expensive equipment, but many feel the pull of wild places, feel compelled to venture up mountains and into forests even if they don't have a GPS or a head torch or a Gore-Tex waterproof jacket. The unlucky few end up as Mountain Rescue statistics for internet trolls to crow over. But they respond to the same urges, conscious and unconscious, that had driven me to this beautiful and lonely place. I closed my eyes and tried to forget my artificial light, warm sleeping bag and sturdy tent waiting for me. To venture here after dark without these things would be taboo, and yet is it not a more honest expression of what it is to be an embodied living creature on planet Earth? Who is to say which of us is the wiser?

True escape from technological systems is impossible. We wouldn't want to escape even if we could, would we? Even the person who comes here without hill gear is wearing shoes and clothes. They probably carry a mobile phone. These technological marvels give us superhuman powers beyond the unaugmented human animal's abilities. We are all cyborgs.

As I gave up and fished my head torch out of my pack, I thought about the tracking device that I would activate soon to ping my location to family, friends and colleagues, and I thought about the smartphone that I was trying to use in a particular and deliberate way, artificially cutting myself off from the internet while taking advantage of its many other miraculous abilities. I had made a decision to use technology deliberately, but did that matter? Had it made any difference? Was I any less of a cyborg for my line drawn uncertainly in the sand, or was I just as enmeshed as everyone else?

Cool artificial light flooded the landscape and instantly changed its character, washing out the delicate radiance in the sky and rendering everything outside the light's cone of influence as absolute blackness. Within it, all was etched in blinding clarity and sharp shadows.

As I busied myself stomping around looking for some flat ground, and then getting out my tent and unrolling the dew-damp flysheet for another night under a starry sky, I forgot all about the vaster world outside my torch beam for a while. I could see everything, and yet my everything had become infinitely smaller. I was an embodied human being in a magical landscape. I was also a cybernetic organism, partly embedded in a cybernetic reality, along with everyone I had ever known. When I turned my torch off for a few minutes before diving into my tent, and the stars came alive again for me to gaze at and wonder at, I told myself that both were ultimately OK things to be.

Chapter 11

Day 18: 23 February 2019

It was a big day through the An Teallach area. I made rapid progress down the first section of the trail towards Shenavall, although the cloud cover became thicker and a few drops of drizzle started to spray in on the wind, which was now very strong and blowing in from behind me. When I reached Strath na Sealga, I didn't make the detour to Shenavall after all – I took the hill track directly out of the valley, as I had decided that I wanted to make tracks to the bunkhouse where my parcel was waiting. Some feral goats watched me as I climbed. The mountain wall of An Teallach looked impressive but was largely free of snow, just a few patches left on the highest slopes.

I descended to Dundonnell and then began the steep climb back up over the next hill. This section felt quite tough – something about the combination of slogging uphill with a pack that never seems to get any lighter, the pinch of my shoulder straps, and boots that felt as if they were made of lead. Flagging, I made it down the incredibly steep descent.

I didn't know what to expect from the Forest Way Bunkhouse. It was set just off the main road from Inverness to Ullapool, in a place called Lael – a thinly dispersed village strewn in a long line between riverbank and A road. I had descended from the high ground to get there, and at less than forty metres above sea level this was the lowest point I'd visited for quite a while. As dusk fell I felt hemmed in by the closeness of the glen.

An older couple who lived in the house next to the bunkhouse greeted me. I soon learnt that they were the parents of Iain, who ran the place and who had been so helpful during my preparations for the trip. After shaking my hand, the man went looking for my supply parcel, then carried it out for me into the yard where the bunkhouse stood apart from the house – 'I'll no hear of you carrying the parcel yourself as well as that huge pack.' A welcoming golden glow streamed out through the bunkhouse kitchen window; it seemed that I would have company.

'There are just two staying tonight, plus yourself,' Iain's father said as he opened the door with a shoulder, straining under the weight of my supply box. 'A couple up from England. Munro-baggers. You'll get on, I'm sure.'

I dumped my pack on the ground and followed him into the porch. Laughter inside was suddenly cut short and I felt a wall of warm air hit me as I breached the airlock and stepped from the porch into the open-plan living room and kitchen area.

A tall young man clad in hiking trousers and a red fleece was standing at the hob with his back turned to me, a swirl of delicious-smelling steam rising from the wok as he prodded at it with a spatula. He turned and gave me a wave; I saw tightly curled blond hair and an angular, chiselled face. A slightly older woman, perhaps my age, was reclining in one of the comfy chairs a few metres away, thumbing through a magazine and taking a sip from a glass of something that looked alcoholic. I didn't like to make assumptions about people, but the label 'mountain athlete' immediately sprang to mind; she looked like someone who could climb eight grades harder than me and took her mountaineering seriously. By the look of her expensive technical attire, she earnt more than I did too – either that or she was also a gear reviewer. I waved back at them both, feeling dirty and scruffy and a little intimidated.

'Seb,' the bloke said over his shoulder, and the woman introduced herself as Claire.

Iain's father deposited my cardboard box on the floor and took me through a few items of housekeeping, then left. I stepped back outside for a moment to haul my pack from where it had been leaning against the wall, and dragged it into the bunkhouse, clattering and banging.

'Seb's making dinner,' Claire said, eyeing my muddy pack. 'Chicken stir fry. There's loads. Want some?'

My stomach growled audibly. Hiker hunger had become an all-consuming preoccupation for me, and I wasn't going to turn down free food.

***

The stir fry was excellent. Apparently Seb and Claire had been expecting several friends to join them, but they'd cancelled at the last minute due to the poor conditions and therefore it was double portions for all.

I could feel tiredness catching up with me, and wanted nothing more than to retreat to the bunk room to unpack my supply box and make a start on planning logistics for the next stage of the trail, but I also craved conversation.

'So,' Claire said as she scooped the last of her food from the bowl, 'Cape Wrath? You haven't picked the best season to do it in winter conditions, have you?'

She had a crisp English accent, carefully calibrated to be not quite posh.

'It's refreshing to talk to someone who understands that I *wanted* snow and ice,' I said with a laugh. 'Most people just think I'm a bit odd for walking at this time of year but lucky with the mild weather. How about yourselves? Up for some Munros?'

'Yes, Seb and I are up An Teallach tomorrow. Aren't we, darling?'

'Hm?'

Seb had picked up the magazine Claire had been reading earlier, and as he flicked through it I couldn't help noticing a familiar cover design, taglines 'the best of 2018' and 'perfect winter walks' emblazoned across a snowy mountain landscape. This issue of *The Great Outdoors* was the most recent release, containing the results of the year's TGO Awards. As a judge in the awards, I'd put dozens of hours into this issue, from product testing to proofreading, number crunching to communications. And I felt a reflexive echo of anxiety as I looked at it – a distinct physical sensation. *That's weird,* I thought. I was used to feeling anxious when faced with an overflowing inbox or a hundred notifications on Twitter, but this was something new.

'Yep, An Teallach,' Seb said, unaware of my momentary turmoil. 'Classic tick. One of the few hills I've done that Claire hasn't.' He focused on me. 'You'll have walked past it today, right? Not much snow, I take it?'

We chatted about conditions for a bit, and I started to pick up more hints about my bunkhouse companions. Claire was a significantly more experienced mountaineer and backpacker than her partner. Both had high-paying and high-stress jobs in London. Neither was thrilled about conditions this winter.

'I really think you've got to grab these opportunities with both hands these days,' Claire said with an expansive gesture encompassing the bunkhouse kitchen and all the hills around us outside. 'I mean, Seb and I don't get much time off, and certainly not together. Conditions are crap now, but next time they might not be. You've got to keep doing the drive up, haven't you? It's worth it when it comes together. You've got to keep trying, keep reaching for opportunities.'

'I guess you do,' I said, 'although it gets disheartening when you live in England. The grass isn't necessarily greener on the other side, though.' I told them about my years living in Glen Coe with the mountains on my doorstep – years in which I started to take the mountains for granted and stopped appreciating them.

'I can understand that,' Claire said. 'The first time I hiked the Haute Route Pyrenees, it was a dream come true. The second time didn't feel as special. Perhaps the novelty wears off.'

'You've hiked the Haute Route Pyrenees? What's it like?'

The conversation turned to the big routes we'd all done and the ones we wanted to do. Seb was the least experienced of the three of us; he had hiked several English long-distance trails, and had ticked off quite a few Lake District hills, but hadn't done anywhere near as much in Scotland – 'Pressures of my job, you know.' Claire was a highly experienced rock climber and alpinist who had only recently begun to dip her toes into the more subtle charms of hill-bagging and backpacking.

Lists, summits, ticks, aspirations – it was a fast-moving conversation. Before too long, Seb seemed to expend his supply of sociability, and withdrew back to his magazine, occasionally nodding in response to questions from his partner as he thumbed the pages.

'Don't mind him,' Claire said. 'He needs his downtime.'

'That's OK,' I said. 'I think I recognise a fellow introvert.'

Seb smiled, then hesitated. 'It's not really that. I suffer from anxiety. Quite badly, in fact. I'm learning how to be open with it. The mountains help.'

Claire smiled back at him briefly. Then she was looking at me, and something in her expression, suddenly very still and searching, told me that she had seen something.

***

I hauled my supply box and rucksack into the bunk room. Seb and Claire's kit had expanded to fill the available space. The room looked like the untidy store cupboard of a gear shop, with an explosion of technical fabrics, backpacks, water bottles, crampons, ice axes, and other mountaineering paraphernalia covering almost every surface. I wondered how we would have found room for everyone (and their gear) if Seb and Claire's friends had turned up.

I staked my claim to one of the top bunks and began my own gear explosion. Most of my stuff was dry, luckily, although I'd already hung my damp waterproofs up in the porch (my waterproofs seemed to be permanently damp on this trip whether or not it had been raining). I was sitting on the floor and had just begun rifling through my supply box when the door creaked open and I saw Seb's tall but slightly stooped figure pass through, blocking out the bright light from the kitchen just beyond.

'Hey,' he said. 'Just come to plug my phone in.'

'Sure.' I moved my pack out of the way of the sockets, and he bent down, charger and cable in hand. *Bing*, his phone bleeped.

He stood there for a moment more, looking at me with an expression caught somewhere between indecision and fear. Suddenly he looked extremely young, younger even than my earlier estimated twenty-five or so.

'Look, Claire asked me to have a word with you. It's a bit awkward, actually.'

Seb squatted down so he was closer to my level, but didn't look directly at me. 'Claire thought she saw a reaction from you about the magazine we'd been reading. She's good at this – she's become an expert at figuring out what's in my head, when I need to talk and when I need time to myself.' Another hesitation. 'She realised that you were one of the writers. In the magazine. Then she worked out who you are – she's read your blog and gets your email newsletter. You were in a couple of the other issues of *TGO* in the lounge too. I guess she put two and two together.'

'What about?'

'About anxiety.' He met my eyes for the first time since entering the room, and behind the hesitation and embarrassment I thought I saw an honest wish to help. 'Look, we don't mean to pry, and tell me to sod off if you like. But I've found that it's good to talk about this stuff, and she thought I should have a quiet word with you. If you want, of course. Maybe my perspective can help.'

My instinct was to brush this away, say I didn't know what he was talking about.

'Claire says it's obvious you've been suffering from anxiety for some time,' Seb continued. 'Your tweets, your newsletter and so on. She saw the same in me before I did. I've learnt a lot about it since then. It's different for everyone, of course, but for me it's linked to imposter syndrome and taking on more work than I can manage, which keeps me too stressed to think about more important long-term priorities I'm ignoring. Displacement, basically, laced with a strong dose of fear that the work will run out. This just makes things worse, and then it snowballs. Being a freelance financial consultant can be hell.' His smile was watery. 'The stupid thing is that I love my job. Anxiety doesn't care about that, though.'

'For me it's the internet,' I said before I'd even made up my mind that I was going to have this conversation. 'The endlessness of it. All the rubbish on Twitter. The thirty or forty emails I have to sort through every morning over breakfast – which to delete, which to think about later, which just sit there ruining my morning until I make a decision and then agonise over how to reply. Things used to be simpler, I'm sure of it.'

Seb was shaking his head. 'Things were never simpler. Maybe you were just younger and had fewer responsibilities. One thing I've learnt is that it's easy to point the finger at some convenient external factor when trying to pin down anxiety triggers. Especially if you're trying to do it without help. The real triggers are good at masking themselves.'

'Maybe you're right.'

'Listen, I don't really know anything about you,' Seb said. 'It's different for everyone. What I will say is that you should keep an open mind. Claire told me that she wouldn't be surprised if you should be looking to your work – maybe you've been taking too much on, or maybe you're in the wrong job.'

I thought about that for a moment. 'I love my job too.'

'It's possible to love something and for it to still trample all over your mental health.' He picked himself off the floor and brushed some dust off his trousers. 'Just think about what I've said, OK?'

***

Day 19: 24 February 2019

The steep climb from Inverlael up through the woods and over to Glen Douchary was what is known in the hiking community as 'an utter bastard'. Despite the clear blue skies and sunshine, I just wasn't feeling it. Steep switchbacks led through a maze of pine trees that all looked exactly the same, and I began to feel tired almost straight away under the kiloton weight of my newly refilled pack, straining at the seams with all the food I'd crammed into it from my Inverlael resupply box. My shoulders weren't as sore, because I'd perfected the optimum use of the chest strap to take some of the force away from those thin shoulder straps, but now the strain seemed to be transmitted directly to my feet instead. *I suppose there are days when something has just got to ache,* I thought as I gasped and sweated at yet another bend in the gravel track, wincing at shooting pains in the soles of both feet. *Today it's my sodding feet.*

Soon I was above the forestry. Looking back every couple of minutes when I stopped to wheeze, I caught increasingly magnificent views of An Teallach on the horizon. I'd walked beneath it on my journey to Inverlael. The mountain had looked gaunt and forbidding from directly below, all contrast and hard angles between rock and what snow remained, but from over here the mountain looked calmer and somehow at ease with itself: a clutch of abstract pyramidal forms thrust up into the blue from indistinct copper-haze moorland. Given enough distance, chaos weaves harmony, pain becomes memory, and that thought sustained me on the long traverse around the flank of Beinn Bhreac while every footstep seemed to stab more than the last and I wondered if I were spiralling back into the hatezone again.

After the track disappeared, I had a lengthy pathless section to negotiate above Glen Douchary. The guidebook recommended contouring at about 520 metres. As with other pathless sections of the trail, I found faint traces of tracks here and there, even a few cairns pointing the way, and soon I descended to a cluster of ruins beside the confluence of two rivers. Something about this place whispered to me. The broad-bottomed glen climbed gently east for a few kilometres towards the massive canyon of Cadha Dearg, a shadowed corrie rimmed with crags suspended beneath the peaks of Seana Bhràigh and Meall Glac an Ruighe. Though only just on the other side of the hill from a major road, this place breathed isolation and silence.

Beyond the rough deer grass marking the land at the confluence where humans had once dwelt, boulders rich with centuries of moss and lichen lay strewn throughout the heather. They had probably not moved since they were deposited there by the glacier that had lived and died in this glen millennia ago. Centuries before I'd been born, people had lived in the houses whose raw materials had now become part of the landscape once more: a pile of stones here, a tumbledown wall there, a hummocky line ten yards long in the moss. I was a man walking through this landscape for fun, or something like it. I could no more put myself into the shoes of these people than I could put myself into the unknowable mind of the glacier itself, or the wondrous spirits it had conjured up in myths so ancient that the stories themselves now left no trace.

When I opened my water bottle to take a swig, I noticed a tiny shrimp darting about in the bottom, and I watched it for a moment, observed its minute limbs as they moved and the creature swam. *How long had that been in there?* My first instinct was to tip the water out and refill my bottle, but I decided to let the shrimp be.

I hiked on. The River Douchary was a peaceful watercourse as I found it, but I saw evidence that a powerful torrent had surged through perhaps only weeks before and carved up the riverbanks, hacking great cake-slices of turf from the ground and leaving muddy islets strewn at intervals in the current. The deluge had created a new, lower course for the river, leaving the old pebbly bed exposed and dry at a higher level. As I splashed across the new channel, stones shifted loosely underfoot, as if they had not yet had time to acquire the bedded-in firmness of a mature watercourse. The far bank was a bisected peat cliff about three or four metres high. The flood had sliced through it with precision and now the moist black peat eroded directly into the water, revealing the white bones of prehistoric trees a metre or two below the modern-day surface and the root strata beneath that. There had been no time for moss or lichen to grow on these trunks. The light of a younger sun had blessed them thousands of years before, and for all the aeons in between they had been sealed safe beneath the peat, awaiting the moment when some savage flood would expose them to a different world. I stared at the bleached fragments in something like rapture. Would life colonise these old bones now, mosses and lichens exploding through the cell structures of long-dead organisms, or would the sudden transition from darkness to light shock them into dust?

***

I followed the Douchary for some kilometres. This was a tough but fascinating section of trail. After I passed through the remains of the ghost forest, the river funnelled itself into a gorge that continued for a long way until it spilled into a network of other gorges. I struggled along the east bank until a patchwork path appeared amongst the bushes of heather. Remnant Caledonian forest clung to the banks of the ravine below me, ancient birches and pines sprouting out of the rocks where the deer couldn't reach, becoming more numerous and densely packed as I gradually descended, following the exposed deer tracks on the side of the gorge.

This place felt very wild, and yet I knew that it hadn't always been like this. A map of the area from between 1583 and 1596 showed many settlements along the line of this route. No trace of them was now visible apart from the austere ruins I'd passed at the confluence of the streams. The peat had consumed everything.

I soon lost the route entirely. What vague path remained had vanished beneath the heather. The guidebook wasn't much help, and I didn't have the benefit of prior knowledge – on my previous CWT I'd taken the easier route from Ullapool. This region was marked on the map as Innis Dhonnchai. As I descended (too far north from the main route heading to Loch an Daimh, I later realised) I found myself scrambling down steep banks of scree and a miniature rainforest of ferns towards what looked like impenetrable trees. Invisible through the undergrowth below, water crashed from pool to pool. As I slithered downwards, trying not to dig in too much with my trekking poles to avoid damaging the delicate vegetation, I wondered if I'd made a mistake. The slope was getting steeper and I suddenly visualised myself losing my footing and sliding all the way down.

At the bottom, I found the bones of a hind strewn over a beach of pebbles. Pine boughs moved and sighed above me in a breeze I could not feel. The rocky sides of the ravine were coated in mosses, lichens, ferns and herbs, a carpet so thick that it pillowed the hard corners of the rocks and muffled all sound, hushing the river's voice. The expectant quiet, and the close walls, made me think of the nave of a church. A sacred and separate realm. A place distinct from the open heather and cleared settlements and ghost forests above.

Without consciously seeing or hearing it, I sensed the presence of a wild creature. An instant later a dipper flashed from rock to rock before diving beneath the water and emerging a metre or more away with a tiny invertebrate tweezered in its bill. The small brown bird landed on a root half in and half out of the water, shook silvery droplets from its plumage, and then looked at me for a second before flying into the deep shade beneath trees further up the gorge. Light from above dappled on the ever-moving surface of the water. Something, I felt absolutely certain, had been communicated to me in that instant, but I felt too stupid and oblivious to understand what I had been shown. It slipped from my grasp like the quicksilver of the whispering rapids. I felt a momentary but devastating sensation of failure, of a chance that would never come again – like a dream containing an entire lifespan that dissolves upon waking, leaving only a profound sense of loss.

A deer track took me back out the other side. When I looked back, I could see little but the swaying tops of the pines and the purple-black twigs of winter birches. There was no trace of the hidden gorge and the dipper's capsule universe.

***

A noise dragged me from deep sleep. For long seconds I had no idea where or even who I was. My eyes felt as if they were filled with glue. When I succeeded in opening them, I could see no more than the faintest grey glow above me, and I groped for my glasses, suddenly entangled in my sleeping bag. My inflatable mat creaked beneath me. *What the hell was that noise?*

I heard it again – the unmistakable sound of a knock on the bothy door. The hairs rose on the back of my neck and I instinctively tried to press myself down against the sleeping platform, to make myself invisible.

The Schoolhouse is one of those bothies that has a reputation for being creepy, with its old disused school desks and a blackboard up on one wall of the main room. I'd written a short message on the blackboard with the provided chalk, of course. It felt like a requirement, a token ritual to ward off bad trail-luck. The bothy was cold too; it's one of the few bothies with no fireplace. I'd made myself at home in the warmer (and less watchful) left-hand room, but there was still a certain presence there, and I'd felt on edge as I drifted off to sleep.

Knock knock.

The door opened with an almighty groan, there were footsteps in the entrance hall, and then I heard someone say 'There's a chalkboard! And Alex has been here.'

I recognised that voice. It was Skye!

The footsteps got closer and then the inner door opened. Light from a head lamp blinded me as the visitor stamped into the room, and the familiar long-distance hiker fragrance of bog water and wet socks reached my nostrils. I sat up and reached for my own head torch, then clicked it on to a low beam.

'Is that you, Skye? What time is it?' I said groggily.

'Whoa! Alex? You're still on the trail?'

'What *time* is it?' I said again, and this time reached for my watch. It was six o'clock in the morning. *What kind of lunatic is on the trail at six o'clock in the morning at this time of year?*

'I know, it's early,' he said, and there was a hint of pride in his voice. 'Hoping to do a lot of miles today.'

Memory came back as sleep left me. I remembered the last time I'd seen Skye, back at Corryhully bothy the other side of Knoydart. I'd sensed that this young man felt the need to prove himself. Hiking from Land's End to John o'Groats in the middle of winter, via the Cape Wrath Trail, is not the way an average sixteen-year-old would choose to spend their time.

I sat up in my sleeping bag as Skye dumped his pack on the floorboards and ran a hand through his unruly straw-coloured hair. I couldn't see much in the dim light of our torches. I'd set mine to its lowest burn to save battery, and I imagined Skye had done the same. The dull LED beams cast pools of bluish light that refracted from the old empty bottles lined up on the top shelf of the bothy, and Skye was just a shadow as he stood there, as if the very idea of another hiker on this trail in February could be no more than a mirage.

'I read your note at Maol Bhuidhe,' I said to him. 'Heck of a job getting across Knoydart. And the rest of it.'

'The last few days have been easy enough,' he said with a shrug, 'but yeah, it's been a bit sketchy in places. I know what you mean now. When you told me about river crossings back in Glenfinnan I didn't have a clue. I went to Kinbreak bothy, and the river came up overnight – it was bloody waist deep!'

I felt incredibly happy to see him. The terms of my solitude had made many things clear to me, even though these lessons were not always the ones I had expected to learn. Personal interaction is cheap in the twenty-first century – so cheap that the glut of messages and emails in everyday life can feel like a burden. Remove that abundance, replace it with a few in-person interactions, and perspective is restored. Bonds form quickly on the trail and in the mountains. Perhaps that is doubly true on a trail as lightly trodden as this one in the darker months of the year.

'I thought you'd be days ahead of me by now, given the pace you were going,' I said. 'All those big days and early starts.'

'Yeah, I've been having foot problems.' A shrug. 'I've had to take some time off. I'm trying to make up for lost time. There is one other guy on the trail I've seen,' he told me. 'Class of winter 2019, am I right? Seems crazy as the trail is so much better than I've heard it can be in summer. No crowds, no ticks—'

'Actually, I have seen ticks,' I cut in.

He looked shocked at that. We chatted about conditions. I rambled on about how summer-like the trail was, how different it would be in an average year, but my young friend had no experience of Scotland in winter. I didn't know if he could visualise the images that were filling my own mind as I described driving blizzards and steep snow slopes – the beauty and romance and peril of winter.

I could tell that he was itching to be off, itching to get ahead, driven by that same metronomic force that was also propelling me towards Cape Wrath, so I said goodbye, and off he went. If the CWT class of winter 2019 consisted of me, Skye and one other guy I'd never met, what did that mean? Was our experience more special for being shared with almost nobody else, or less? As I lay back in my sleeping bag and switched off my torch, letting complete blackness reassert itself, I could not decide.

Chapter 12

Day 21: 26 February 2019

Thirty-six hours after leaving Schoolhouse bothy, I was descending steep ground from Bealach Trallgil on the edge of Assynt. Assynt is one of the Cape Wrath Trail's true marvels. Most of Assynt lies to the west, interrupting the logical line of the CWT with a bewitching swathe of lochs and rivers and wild land. Look at the map and you could be forgiven for wondering why the CWT veers so far east to Glen Oykel at all when the direct line through the heart of Assynt looks so much better. The truth is that there's so much water there, so many lochans and difficult river crossings, that you'd need a boat to do it comfortably. There may be possible Cape Wrath Trail variants through Assynt's heartland, but they're too obscure to have made it into any of the guidebooks or maps.

The previous day had not been a good one. My mood had been upbeat as I left the bothy, but soon deteriorated upon entering Glen Oykel in the wind and rain, and I remembered why this had been the worst section of my 2015 CWT. In the foreground had been numbered fishing pools along the River Oykel, where rich clients paid to take salmon from a tamed river. In the distance, I saw a devastated commercial timber crop where trees had been strip-mined by machines. Most of the Highlands is a managed landscape, of course, but the Cape Wrath Trail is clever at disguising this fact and presenting an illusion of bewitching natural beauty. Glen Oykel broke the illusion.

Bealach Trallgil, the high pass beneath the mountains of Conival and Ben More Assynt, is one of the trail's high points and a difficult pass in poor conditions. I had not found it easy last time; in fact, it had thrashed me, and I'd become badly lost on the other side of the col in mist and driving rain.

There was a strange sense of dissonance as I picked my way down from the bealach. It was a feeling that had been growing in me over the last few days – a sense of two timelines layered over one another. Two hikes, 2015 and 2019, somehow coexisting, as if the gulf of time between them had collapsed and I had become unable to distinguish between the two. Although I walked in good visibility with dry grass underfoot and the sun on my cheek, the path clearly visible ahead, part of me relived that earlier experience, at first scrambling down steep cliffs I'd somehow wandered on to and then floundering around in a bog somewhere several hundred metres to my left, soaked to the skin and flirting with hypothermia and about to tackle the most dangerous river crossing of the entire trip. That had been June. It had felt more like February. Today it was February and felt like June.

Thanks to better visibility, I avoided the cliffs and the bog and the nasty river crossing this time, and found a comfortable path weaving between rock outcrops down towards Inchnadamph. This section felt chilled out, almost benign. At one point, in warm hazy sunshine, I looked west to see a group of hinds watching me, the outline of Canisp forming a mighty backdrop some miles distant amongst other hills receding in blue misty planes to the sea.

I crossed the River Traligill at the proper crossing and descended almost to Inchnadamph, but didn't go all the way down to the village, as there was no reason for me to go there – the hotel and bunkhouse were closed for the winter, and besides, I had no wish to stop for the night just yet. The day was too sunny and glorious, the urge to find a fine spot for a wild camp high in the hills too strong. Instead of turning left to the village, as I'd done in 2015 with water squelching in my shoes and clothing soaked, I turned right. This path led to Bealach na h-Uidhe, the last major high point on the CWT and a portal to one of the finest wild mountain landscapes in the Highlands. Behind me and a couple of hundred metres below, the waters of Loch Assynt glittered in the afternoon sun, and the houses that clustered at the head of the loch looked inconspicuous, almost apologetic that they might be intruding. But this place felt nothing like Glen Oykel. Despite the lack of trees, there was no sense of nature scraped down to the bone. A soft graphite line of smoke rose pencil-thin from the chimney of one of the houses, barely dissipating in the still air.

As I climbed uphill, breathing hard and breaking a sweat in the sunshine, I soon realised that another hiker was coming up behind me: a figure with red top, green pack and scrawny frame powering uphill at an improbable rate. I could hear the click, click of trekking poles scudding off rocks, provoking my own dormant competitive streak. Without consciously ordering my legs to speed up, I found myself hiking faster uphill, occasionally effecting a casual glance over my shoulder. The oncomer kept coming on. A bead of sweat trickled down my forehead, dangled ponderously from my eyebrow in front of my field of vision, then dripped on to the trail in front of me. I kept going. The hiker was gaining on me so rapidly that I might as well have been standing still.

After five minutes of this, I muttered 'This is ridiculous' to myself and stopped, huffing and puffing, before fumbling for my camera in its bag (stopping to pretend to take a photo is a time-honoured way of grabbing a stealthy rest when you're walking uphill).

'Hey, Alex!'

I looked around. It was Skye, striding with ease along the uneven track heading up into the corrie. I put my camera back in its bag as he drew adjacent. 'What are you doing behind me again?' I asked him. 'I can't work out how I keep overtaking you.'

'I am not going to lie, one of my main challenges on this trail has been evading my parents,' he said with a serious tone as he fell into step just behind me.

'*Evading* them?'

'Yeah, I've had to turn off my inReach tracker so that they can't follow me. It's bloody embarrassing.'

'I feel like I'm missing some context.'

He explained that his parents had been following him at a distance and staying in B&Bs near the trail. They had been keeping tabs on his location thanks to his regular inReach pings, and frequently accosted him to demand he joined them for pub lunches.

'Which always sounds lovely,' Skye added, 'but it costs half a day and I'm brutally behind schedule as it is, even with my three o'clock starts.'

'Three o'clock … in the morning?'

'Yeah. Three o'clock starts, pub lunches, and an ankle that keeps getting worse. This trail has been a lot harder than I bargained for.'

I laughed out loud. I couldn't help myself. 'Sorry,' I said immediately. 'It just sounds so bizarre.'

'Anyway, I've switched off my inReach tracker now. Incognito for a bit. Maybe that'll get my mum and dad off my back.' He let out a sigh that I thought held a trace of self-mockery. 'It's just so embarrassing for a hiker. My parents have been slowing me down a lot. It's been a pain, to be honest.'

I knew it was trail bravado, or maybe he was just fooling around, but something in his words reminded me of what it felt like to be sixteen and take so much for granted.

'You might miss your parents one day, you know.'

'I like to be alone,' he went on. 'It's why I came out here in winter. I bet you don't have to put up with parents watching your every move.'

'My dad died last year, actually. It tends to change your perspective on a few things.'

I hadn't meant to say it. Now that I had, I regretted the cheap shot. Skye was silent for a moment, then he said, 'Shit, sorry to hear that, mate. I didn't mean … '

'Don't worry about it. My satellite tracker is rubbish anyway. It only works half the time. To be honest I think my dad would have told me to trade the damn thing for a bottle of whisky at the first opportunity.'

Skye chortled, and the sudden tension disappeared. I found myself laughing too and I realised that I needed this release, this defusing of a constant low-level grief that had never been far beneath the surface for my whole journey. Even though Dad's death had been a year ago, the loss had felt very near, and very raw, in this extended period of solitude. I'd brooded about it, been anxious about it, obsessed over it, and, yes, cried about it (once, in Hannah's arms, the night after his death), but I'd never *laughed* about it. Dad and I had laughed about plenty of things together. Perhaps it was right that I'd come far enough now that I was able to laugh about this. I felt suddenly grateful for Skye and his earnest wish to be taken seriously.

As we hiked uphill into Fleodach Coire towards the sunlit slopes above, the conversation veered to other topics, and I gained a fascinating glimpse into Skye's life. I got the impression that he held himself to incredibly high standards – not just as a hiker but in other areas too. He described himself as 'seriously' behind on his A levels (his parents expected him to get A*s) and already had several unis lined up – 'Oxford maybe, or a uni in Scotland, to be close to the mountains.' Incredibly, he had continued to run his eBay businesses while on the trail, making and selling custom ultralight hiking gear and buying and selling coins. Just listening to him made me feel exhausted.

'This is only the first step, of course,' he said passionately. 'If I can hike the Cape Wrath Trail in winter – and apart from Knoydart it hasn't actually been that bad – then I can do pretty much anything I want. The PCT in winter, maybe.'

'You're doing amazingly well,' I said, and I meant it; I could not have done what he was doing when I was sixteen. 'Bear in mind that this isn't a typical winter, though. Winter in the Highlands usually lasts a lot longer than this. In the past I have been ice climbing on Ben Nevis in May.'

'That was a long time ago, though, surely,' he said.

'Not that long. Nine years … '

'That's a long time.'

I laughed. 'Don't let anything I say put you off. You can do whatever you want. You've proved that much already.'

We parted ways in the upper corrie, just before the path dropped down beneath a pair of glistening lochs hidden in the folds of the landscape. The light was starting to soften, bronzing the rippling grass on the hills. Skye wanted to push on to Glencoul bothy that night – quite a step, and it would involve negotiating the challenging gorge of the Leitir Dhubh in darkness, missing the spectacular view of Eas a' Chual Aluinn, the highest waterfall in Britain. I told him that he'd be better off camping with me and making his way through the wonderful Assynt high country in daylight, but he wanted to make for the bothy. As I started to look for somewhere to camp, he sped away from me with a parting 'Great day!' towards the bealach in the distance.

I looked for a pitch for my tent amongst the knolls and lochans. Eventually I came across a fine, well-drained pitch on an elevated prow with fine views of Glas Bheinn and Bheinn Uidhe above me. The sun set through layers of haze on the western horizon while I pounded tent pegs into the stony ground. The temperature dropped as the sun failed and I put on my down jacket before making the five-minute walk to the burn for water.

Later, as I lay beneath the dew-heavy flysheet of my tent, I wrote in my journal:

This is easily the best camp so far on the CWT – and I've had some good ones. Silence apart from the distant roar of a waterfall, and splendid isolation high on a mountain in Assynt. Four days left to Cape Wrath, all being well …

***

Day 22: 27 February 2019

There are a few places on the CWT that define the trail, that give it the power it holds over us, that resonate strongly in the memory down the years. Some of those places are in Knoydart, or in Torridon; one is in Assynt, crossing the Bealach na h-Uidhe. This pass, at just above 600 metres, is the last bit of significant high ground on the trail. The path rose from Fleodach Coire to a gentle bealach of grey scree and then suddenly revealed what was hidden on the other side: a treeless world of folded horizons and rocky spurs, of the corners of lochans, of dark hollows and the suggestions of depths plunging out of sight to inlets and fjords that can only be imagined. The world beyond this bealach seemed to occupy more space than had been allocated to it on the map.

Warm sunshine greeted me at the bealach, but the wind blowing in from the north almost made me put my jacket back on after the stuffy ascent. I found myself transfixed for a moment by a moss colony growing amongst the rocks: delicate shades of green, from aqua to almost yellow, and textures from soft fronds to what looked like the defensive spines of some desert plant. A few flowers had started to unfurl – tiny pink planetoids held up on stalks. This micro-habitat was coming back to life. Below the bealach, in the enchanted world beyond, two hinds grazed in the sunshine. They ambled away from me as I began to make my way down the rough path on the other side.

I resisted the urge to hike quickly. This was a place to be savoured, to be experienced in full – and besides, I knew from past experience that it was easy to miss the pathless descent into the ravine. I spent as long as I could just sitting beside one of the lochans and looking into the waters, my mind empty. This jewel felt huddled and hidden, secluded within a hollow, and I grappled for a word to describe what I intuitively felt at this place. A light breeze feathered the water, but as I stared unfocused into it suddenly it was not water at all – down was up, and the sky's inversion in frosted blackness beneath me was an entire world paused in time and cupped there by the mountain. The disorienting perception shift lasted only a moment, but the sense remained that this place was a portal to some other realm. A spray of boulders at the narrowest point bore an echo of that feeling as I turned my head to look at them – not islets, or rocks with their toes in a peaty puddle, but particles of grit in the eye of another world.

Time breathed again as I picked up my pack and prepared to get going. Although I no longer felt any reflexive need to do so, I made a deliberate point of checking my phone for signal, perhaps to prove to myself that I'd changed. The screen glowed. Zero bars. I pushed a button and it was just a black slab of glass, greasy with fingerprints, but it was also a human artefact that would not decompose for a million years or more. The dissonance in this place could hardly have been more jarring.

For a moment I fantasised about throwing it into the portal as a sacrifice. What strange gods would demand such an offering? In our cybernetic reality we carry around shards of our souls in our pockets, imbue them with potent spiritual power. Although few of us would admit it, research suggests that the smartphone is the single most important object that most of us own – certainly the object with the most hold on us. In 2017, a study found that even a switched-off smartphone can demand attention and reduce ability to think.[1] I wondered if this was still true for me now. If I were to throw my iPhone into that portal, cast away my digital horcrux, would I be throwing my soul in with it?

I didn't do any such thing, of course. A chunk of lithium and silicon and glass in the bottom of a Scottish lochan didn't bear thinking about. Its battery might corrode and leach chemicals into the water, which would be bad enough, but the object itself might still be lying there after the glaciers had come and gone ten times, a hundred times, after our civilisation had left nothing but an indelible stratum of waste metres beneath the earth. I recoiled from that glimpse into deep time. But wherever this phone ended up, it would continue its journey through eternity long after I was dust. I was not an innocent party here. By purchasing it, I had helped to create the demand for it to exist, and I was responsible for it now. I used it as a tool; it used me. Ownership went both ways, but I knew that this journey had loosened the hooks it had long lodged in my mind. And I'd gained the perspective to realise that this was not really a parasitic relationship but a symbiotic one.

So I turned away. Perhaps in a sense I had shed something into that black pool after all, and I wondered if I had passed some sort of test, but at the same time I knew that my own preoccupations and anxieties had muscled in on a moment of rare perception in this landscape. I resented that.

***

1 Ward, A.F., Duke, K., Gneezy, A. and Bos, M.W., 'Brain Drain: The Mere Presence of One's Own Smartphone Reduces Available Cognitive Capacity', *Journal of the Association for Consumer Research*, Volume 2, No. 2, University of Chicago Press (published online 3 April 2017), https://www.journals.uchicago.edu/doi/abs/10.1086/691462

Eas a' Chual Aluinn is, the guidebook will inform you, one of the high-lights of the Cape Wrath Trail. It's the highest waterfall in Britain, so by definition it must be a scenic highlight. While undeniably impressive, to me it felt more like scenery than landscape as it came into view – an attractive backdrop rather than a place with a soul of its own, although perhaps that was just a result of the bright, flat lighting, or the cascade's relatively thin flow for the time of year, or my own state of mind. The waterfall streamed down the left wall of the canyon, a ceaseless sweep of water with few obvious terrain features to give it scale.

I picked my way over the rough ground on the other side of the riv-er. Just like the last time I'd walked through this impressive cliff-rimmed canyon, I couldn't stop the music from *The Fellowship of the Ring* playing on loop in my head. The landscape was too brashly cinematic, almost over the top in its magnificence. I felt like a hobbit on a quest. *Perhaps,* I wondered, half-expecting a dragon to soar over the edge of the cliff and perch silhouetted against the blue sky, *this is the sort of place that you have to visit when the stars are right to see it truly.*

My senses felt dulled and frayed, as if they had been burnt out or used up after my moment of searing clarity at the lochan on the hillside above. I would see no more inner glimpses today. My perception would be as two-dimensional as the blue glass of the sea loch, motionless in the calm of an unseasonably warm February afternoon.

***

Like the last leafy branch on an otherwise dead tree, Glencoul bothy was the only habitable part remaining of what had once been a sizeable house. Its green-painted gable end faced me as I walked towards it down the trail, while the much larger main house protruded to the left, chim-ney stacks rising above a pair of wind-stooped trees. Beyond, a few white clouds drifted over the waters of Loch Glencoul. The bothy door was open a crack, so I dumped my pack and poles and stepped in. I wondered if I'd find a message from Skye in the bothy book.

Better than that: I found Skye himself, still cocooned in his sleeping bag in the right-hand room. Light streamed through the window and I couldn't help noticing his possessions strewn everywhere, from stove and food bag to a drone plugged in to a power bank whose LED was blinking, indicating depleted power. He was sitting upright, back leaning against the far wall, dressed in his hiking clothes – waterproof jacket and all – and sleeping bag pulled up to his armpits. He seemed more asleep than awake as I came in, but blinked when he noticed me standing in the doorway.

'Afternoon,' I said. 'Thought you were going to get up before dawn and hike all the way to Kinlochbervie today?'

'Yeah … I arrived at ten o'clock last night, so tired I could hardly bloody stand. Didn't even inflate my sleeping mat or hang my food bag.' He rubbed his chin ruefully. 'Ended up descending that huge gorge in the dark. Didn't see the big waterfall, of course, but I could hear it.'

He looked pale and tired. No wonder, given how hard he'd been pushing himself.

'Are you feeling OK? You don't look too good.'

'Maybe I'm dehydrated. My ankle still isn't great, and I've got a headache. I'm probably not eating enough – just chocolate and biscuits while hiking, really.'

'Those ridiculously early starts won't be helping,' I said. 'Look, we're not far from the end now. If you try to keep up this pace you'll just end up burning yourself out.'

'I guess it isn't a forced march.'

'Maybe even enjoy it! But definitely take a slower day tomorrow.'

He nodded, glanced at his watch, and blinked in surprise. 'It's gone one o'clock anyway. I guess today is a write-off.'

I took another look around the room. There was water in a bottle standing on the edge of the sleeping platform, and his food bag obviously had at least some food in it. I took another look at Skye. Suddenly I wasn't sure I should be leaving him by himself.

'Are you going to be OK?'

'Honestly, I'll be fine. I promise I'll take a short day today and take it easy.'

'Maybe turn your inReach tracker back on too,' I suggested.

After signing the bothy book (Skye hadn't added his own entry yet), I made ready to leave, and Skye started to extricate himself from his sleeping bag.

'Well, I'm going to keep going,' I said. 'I might stop at Glendhu bothy or camp somewhere on the shore a bit further on.'

Skye stood, yawned, stretched, and began gathering his possessions into a pile. 'Yeah, I'll be along soon myself. I'm feeling much better, actually. Hike well. Maybe I'll see you at Glendhu.'

I closed the door behind me and picked up my pack. Ten minutes later, after following the path along the shoreline of the loch and over the river, after pausing to admire the lonely war memorial on the hillside, and after beginning the steep pull up the track that climbed the prow of land separating Loch Glencoul from Loch Glendhu, I looked back to see Skye following behind me almost a kilometre away, his distinctive red jacket flashing in the sun.[2]

I found myself wondering about Skye's relationship with solitude. He obviously craved it – he'd told me himself that he liked to be alone, and that one reason he'd chosen the CWT in winter was to seek solitude, much the same as me. But hiking alone can be hard as well as rewarding. Setbacks and pitfalls cut all the deeper without someone else there to help keep perspective. I knew this all too well. Perhaps Skye and I had found the best balance of solitude and companionship: hiking apart, but helping each other when we needed it. We had laughed together when I needed to laugh, and I'd given him the strength he needed to get out of his sleeping bag and keep going, even if just for a couple of hours before more much-needed rest.

Out there on the trail, where everything is more intense and life itself feels more real, such things are precious.

***

2 The war memorial, the most remote in Scotland, is a tribute to William and Alistair Elliot – two brothers who grew up in the now-empty estate cottage and were both killed in the First World War.

Even as I left Glendhu bothy late in the evening, looking for somewhere else to camp a bit further along, I knew that I'd made a mistake. Glendhu is one of my favourite bothies. It has everything: a beautiful location on the shore of a sea loch, downstairs rooms filled with fascinating knick-knacks visitors had scooped up from the high-tide mark, and a comfortable attic for sleeping in. I'd stayed at Glendhu last time and been woken by the sound of a pony licking the window. This time, however, I found a single can of lager perched on the mantelpiece above the fireplace like an offering. It was just a friendly gesture from the last visitor, of course, or perhaps a gift from the maintenance officer for the next person to come along, but something about it made me turn away. It made me think of summer and overcrowded bothies and litter. Problems I had already acknowledged my own part in.

So I hiked on, looking for somewhere to camp on the shores of the loch, but part of me already knew that I should have stayed at the bothy, should have accepted the offering, and that now something bad would happen. The superstition was ridiculous. I *knew* it was ridiculous, even as I knew that bad luck would follow me down the trail.

There was nowhere to camp for almost four kilometres. The rutted track clung to the steep sides of the loch; cliffs to my right, boulders to my left dropping directly into the water. I kept going as the light began to fail, hoping that soon I'd find a beautiful little grassy meadow, but I didn't find anywhere suitable until the bridge over the Maldie Burn coming down from Loch an Leathaid Bhuain. This was where the trail turned north and climbed up to a pass, and I knew there would be nowhere to camp up there. I either had to find somewhere near the bridge, in an area of hydro access tracks and ground churned up by construction vehicles, or walk for hours into the dark before I'd find a likely pitch. *Should have stayed at the bothy,* I told myself as I dumped my pack and began scanning the rough slopes between burn and loch. At least the weather had remained fine and calm.

The pitch I found was marginal at best, slumped in a knobbly hollow between the remains of a stone wall and a slope dropping down to the loch, but it would have to do. I stamped down the sharp stalks of last year's bracken to make the area as flat as I could, and as I was laying out my tent's flysheet, still sopping with condensation from the night before, I saw something move on my hand. Squinting at it, I saw that it was a tick nymph – impossibly tiny, but unquestionably a tick nymph. Then I saw a second one crawling on the blue cuff of my jacket. Then a third on my sleeve. *Bugger.*

Later, after dark, I lay there zipped up inside my bivvy bag under the flysheet of my tent, hardly daring to move. I'd found ticks on my pack where it had been resting on a patch of heather. I'd found ticks crawling up my trouser legs. I'd found ticks crawling up the underside of my shelter as I'd pitched it, and I'd found more ticks in my spare clothes, on my groundsheet, crawling over the outside of my bivvy bag. A closer look had revealed adult ticks waiting patiently on the ends of the bracken stalks and blades of grass all around me inside my shelter, front legs held out as if in the expectation of an embrace, ready to hook on to the next passing deer (or human). There were ticks quite literally crawling up the walls of my shelter. For the first time on my trip I wished I'd had the sense to pack an inner tent instead of just a groundsheet and bivvy bag.

After a frenzy of checking everything for ticks and flinging the creatures outside my tent, I zipped myself into my bivvy bag to stop them from getting to me, certain that there must be several zipped in with me that I'd been unable to find. They could be crawling in my hair, perhaps, or in the folds of my sleeping bag. Tick nymphs were so small that they were almost impossible to see at the best of times, let alone by the light of a head torch in the dark. I'd still be finding them in my clothes and gear for days, and multiple bites were almost certain. A wave of anxiety coursed over me as I remembered James's long struggle with Lyme disease.

Why were hundreds of ticks active in Scotland in February? I'd never seen anything like it before in my life.

Despite my horror and discomfort, despite my regret at the nice comfortable bothy I could have been snoozing in then and there, I forced myself to see the funny side. This was not the first time I'd been punished by the trail gods for not taking a gift when it was offered, and it wouldn't be the last. I imagined telling my dad about this moment. We'd be sitting in armchairs next to the fireplace, perhaps sipping a dram, and he'd be chuckling about it. So I laughed too. The sound echoed startlingly in the dark. Suddenly things didn't seem so bad.

Chapter 13

Day 23: 28 February 2019

It was the smell that drew me to the ruined boathouse: the unmistakable sweet, cloying stench of decay. My mind was tranquil after an hour or more of off-path navigation through heather and bog, following a series of long, thin lochs through the tessellation of rock and water that was Sutherland. Behind me, the sunlit mountain peaks of Arkle and Foin-aven floated above the landscape as if part of some celestial universe, their sweeping grey slopes too perfect, too sculpted, to have risen from this chaotic place of confused horizons and jumbled-up pools where no path stayed straight for long. After hard work over hills and across rivers, I came at last to the smell of rotting meat coming from the abandoned boathouse beside Loch a' Gharbh-bhaid Beag.

The roof had blown off, and now it lay beside the low stone walls, a rusting and warped pane of corrugated iron almost exactly the same shade of ruddy brown as the heather sprouting up around it. The mortar was flaking away from the stone walls and littered the ground around the boathouse in greening, scab-like flakes. I peered under the corrugated iron where it rested on a boulder at one end. A small stream was flowing under the old roof of the boathouse, and the blotchy lime-green growths of sundew plants clustered over a wet sheen of water on the rocks.

Immediately I saw the source of the smell: the corpse of a hind, partly skeletonised and turning to slime, partly still dressed in fur that looked astonishingly fresh. I couldn't see the animal's face, but I saw the soft flesh of an ear held aloft as if listening for danger outside this desperate shelter into which it had crawled, perhaps with a broken leg after a fall from a crag. The exposed bone of a femur had turned as green as the sun-dew leaves only a few inches away. The bone and the plant were things indivisible from each other. The hind had ceased to be a hind when it had died in this temporary hollow, but had it ever really been a hind at all? I'd never thought of death in that way before. Some might look on the dead hind and feel sadness or pity for it, but just for a moment all I could feel was a profound wonder.

I walked on.

***

The hotel at Rhiconich was shut and silent for the winter, but I found a bar of signal so I gave Hannah a ring and told her that I'd be at Cape Wrath in two days, all being well.

'How's Mum doing?' I asked her. I was anxious about her infected tooth, certain that it would have got worse since we last spoke a few days ago. *Probably much worse,* my anxiety said.

'She's doing OK,' Hannah said. 'The antibiotics seem to be doing the trick, although she's a bit down – you know how it is. She said for you not to ring again until you get to the end. I don't think she wants you worrying about her.'

Again I tried to read between the lines. Hannah's tone told me that Mum was fine – or at least that I had no cause for concern. Part of me had been gearing up to cancel the trip and rush home if necessary. It felt like an inevitable experience just waiting to happen – if not on this trip, in this year, then it was a beast lurking in some more distant corner of my future.

'I'll call or text you when I get to Kinlochbervie,' I told Hannah. 'Not sure where I'm staying yet, but there has to be somewhere to camp, or maybe a B&B. Love you.'

'Love you. I can't wait to have you home.'

After hanging up the phone, I ate the remaining half of the malt loaf squidged into my pocket and started the long plod along the road to

Kinlochbervie in the gathering dusk. My thoughts were calm, formless, as I climbed. I found myself lulled to a walking sleep by the lapping waves on the loch below me. The sun had dropped below a bank of cloud near the western horizon, out over the sea, and god rays streamed up to illuminate the wispy haze covering the sky above. Silence. I passed isolated holiday cottages by the side of the road with their sea views, walked through tiny villages with names like Achriesgill and Rhuvoult. Even the place names sounded different in this part of Scotland. There were thriving communities here, but it had a frontier feel about it.

After about half an hour, I heard the chug-chug-chug of a distant motor and realised that this was the first vehicle I'd heard coming along the road behind me. A squat green van, the sort that people like to convert into tiny mobile homes, soon climbed around the corner towards me. I stepped up on to the grass verge to avoid it. A figure in the driver's seat raised a hand in acknowledgement and I waved back as the van rattled up the incline. I'd taken the van's colour to be uniform khaki at first, but now I saw that it was streaked with either stripes of brown paint or maybe just rust showing through the green. The van passed me, wheezed around the next corner, and was gone.

A few minutes later, I heard it coming back along the road towards me. This time the van drew to a halt opposite and I heard the squeak-squeak-squeak of the driver laboriously winding down his window.

'All right, mate? Want a lift into town?'

An English accent. Northern. I couldn't see much of him in the dim light – just a soft face, eye sockets in shadow, and the suggestion of dark tufts of hair poking out from underneath a cap of some kind. Maybe a beard. I noticed a few items wedged in the gap between the dashboard and the windscreen: an old tin mug covered in stickers, what looked like a paperback book that had been through a washing machine, and a yellow cigarette lighter.

Did I want a lift? It wasn't far to Kinlochbervie, and I preferred the idea of completing the rest of this journey on foot. On the other hand, it was almost dark, I had no idea where I'd stay when I got there, and this driver had taken the trouble to turn around just to see if I wanted a lift.

I realised that I would feel anxious at saying no. So I said yes.

'Hop in, then. I'll open up the back.'

***

I regretted my decision to catch a lift with this guy almost immediately. As I took my pack off and dumped it in the middle of the road – not much chance of another car coming along at this hour – I saw the driver kick open his door and shamble around to the back of the van. He was a short, stooped figure wearing camouflage trousers, a black flat cap, a green woollen jumper, and a khaki waistcoat with lots of pockets, the fabric covered in sewn-on badges that I couldn't see clearly in the dark. There was a powerful smell of weed as he shook my hand. The palm of his leather fingerless glove felt cold and greasy.

'The name's Greg, by the way. Let's get you in the back.' He eyed my pack, resting against the rear wheel. 'Decent rucksack you've got there. On an exped?'

'Something like that,' I said. 'Cheers for the lift. I'm only going as far as Kinlochbervie tonight.'

'Yeah, me too.'

The rear doors of the van opened to reveal a dark interior filled with vague shapes. Before I could say anything, Greg picked up my rucksack, grunted in surprise, and slung it into the back as if it were a sack of potatoes.

'Holy fuck, mate – that weighs a fucking ton.'

Despite my alarm that he might have damaged something in the pack – or possibly something in his van – I couldn't resist a smile.

'All right, then,' he said, 'get in. There's no seat belt, I'm afraid. Not going far though, eh? I'll need to turn round.'

I climbed in. Greg reached past me to flick on a switch, and a single bulb came on, illuminating the interior in a feeble orange glow. He slammed the doors shut behind me and I began fumbling forward, squeezing myself between the wooden bunk on my right and heaps of belongings on my left while items hanging from hooks attached to the ceiling smacked me in the head. There was an old armchair with its back against the partition. I dropped myself into it, dropping further than I thought into an embrace of sagging springs. The chair scraped alarmingly against the floor. I reached forward and grabbed my pack. Suddenly I didn't feel safe letting it out of arm's reach.

'Hold on, mate,' Greg called from the other side of the partition, and then the van took off.

I immediately found that the armchair was not attached to the floor in any way. As the van accelerated, I was flung backwards towards the rear as if the chair were on roller skates. I dug the heels of my boots into the floor and flailed around with my hands to find something to grab on to. All the junk hanging from the ceiling was suddenly in motion, gyrating madly with a noise like a cutlery drawer flung into a tornado.

It was then that I saw the hunting bow. It was a formidable-looking weapon, all sleek black curves and improbable spiky bits, secured firmly to the wall immediately above the camo-pattern bedding lying rumpled on the bunk to my left. While the other items strewn around seemed to have been crammed into the van without thought or care, the bow was clearly a prized possession. My gaze flicked around nervously and soon landed on a quiver of arrows in one corner, wedged in between a Calor gas cylinder and what looked like an anti-tank shell.

What the hell is this?

My first instinct, even as the van took another corner at speed and I was forced to brace myself to avoid smashing into the side, armchair and all, was to laugh. It was just too ridiculous. Every backpacker has a story about hitchhiking; everyone has taken a lift that they ended up regretting. Everyone except me. I'd been hitchhiking for years around Scotland and had never experienced anything strange or uncomfortable. I'd been picked up by plenty of people who weren't interested in chatting, of course, but also many more who proved fascinating sources of conversation – those temporary friends that brighten up life on the trail and help reseat your sense of the good in human nature. But I didn't have a single bad hitchhiking story to tell.

It'll be fine, I told myself. *Just because he likes his army surplus gear and has a hunting bow doesn't mean I'm going to end up murdered in a ditch. I mean, we've all got our hobbies.*

That's what I told myself as I rattled back and forth in the back of a van hurtling towards who knew where in a remote corner of the Scottish Highlands, driven by a strange man called Greg who had specifically gone out of his way to give me a lift. When I'd seen the van coming back towards me I'd assumed that this was just another example of Highland hospitality and friendliness. Now I wasn't so sure.

I took my phone out of my pocket, suddenly very glad to have this lifeline. The display glowed. Zero bars of signal. Where was my satellite tracker? If the worst came to the worst, could I press the SOS button? It was buried somewhere deep in my pack; I didn't even know exactly where I'd stowed it.

What does your instinct tell you? Is this a safe situation, or should you be worried?

I paused and forced myself to be rational. There was no reason to be worried. It was less than a mile to Kinlochbervie. Hannah knew where I was, and she was expecting me to call or text later. I hadn't been separated from my pack. All was well – and yet every sense tingled with danger.

The van bumped and jumped along the road for a few more minutes while I braced myself and tried to hold on to my rucksack. There was just one window I could see out of – a small pane of dirty glass in the back door – and I kept my eye on the darkness rushing past outside, trying to gauge where I was. I saw houses slip past, lit up in splashes of sodium light from widely spaced street lamps. We'd arrived in Kinlochbervie.

I banged on the partition wall behind me. 'I'll get out anywhere that's good for you to stop,' I shouted.

'OK, mate,' he yelled back.

The van came to an abrupt halt with a groan of the brakes and an almighty clatter from all the junk in the back. I heard the driver's door open, then heavy footsteps coming around the side of the van, then the rear doors opened and Greg stood there framed in the dying light of the sky.

'Kinloch-B,' he said. 'Edge of the world.'

***

I stood there in the deserted car park of the petrol station. There were no lights on in the building, which looked like a hybrid between a dilapidated warehouse and a village shop. In fact, there was nobody around at all, but I felt much safer now that I was out of the van. I realised that I was hugging my pack close to my legs as it sat there on the tarmac beside me.

I could see a little more of him now in the faint glow from the street lamp across the road. His camo gear looked old and well-worn, frayed around the hems, whether intentionally or through years of use I could not tell. Something about his aspect suggested military wannabe rather than actual (or ex) military. He was about my height, but slouched as he stood there; his posture suggested someone who spent most of his life sitting down. Several days' worth of patchy, wiry beard mostly concealed a double chin. He looked completely harmless. Suddenly I realised that I'd been overreacting after all; nothing was going to happen. I'd never been in danger. The vibe I got at this precise moment was that he just wanted someone to talk to.

'So,' Greg said, 'what's this trip of yours all about? Been hiking for long?'

I decided there was no harm in a brief conversation. 'A couple of weeks. Cape Wrath Trail, Ardnamurchan to Cape Wrath. I thought it was going to be a winter trip, to be honest, but the weather has had other plans.'

'Yeah, it's fucking great for the time of year, in't it? Of course, it's just weather, not climate, unlike what the mainstream media would have one believe. So much for global warming.' A smug, knowing chuckle.

Something about his tone provoked me. 'This year's different. I've been coming up here for nearly fifteen years, and I've never seen anything like it. Last night I camped on a tick nest, for instance – in February!'

There was a sudden, cold silence.

'Ticks,' Greg said.

I remembered that I'd just spent the last few minutes in the back of his van, sitting in his armchair, and wished I could turn back time to the moment just before I opened my mouth and told him about the tick nest.

'Yes, but I've checked all my gear – no stowaways.' That was a lie. I fully expected to find ten or twenty of them crawling about in my stuff later on.

Greg grunted at that, but seemed satisfied. I decided that the conversation had reached its logical conclusion and moved back a step so that I could lift my pack up on to my shoulders.

'Where to next, then?' Greg asked as I stood there adjusting the straps.

'I'll probably look for a B&B or something,' I said, glancing at my watch. 'Probably too late to find somewhere good to camp now.'

'There's a grand spot for camping down on the beach I know of,' Greg said, drawing closer and dropping his voice to a conspiratorial whisper. 'A lovely little cove, like, hidden away from the road. I've got some beers in the back. Fancy it?'

I detected no danger in his tone, just loneliness, perhaps.

'Thanks, but no,' I said, spreading my hands. 'I told my wife I'd be somewhere with phone signal tonight, and I have to be up early tomorrow.'

Greg nodded and sniffed. 'Just thought I'd ask. If you change your mind … '

'Cheers for the lift,' I said again, and waved as I walked away.

I didn't look back for a minute or two, and when I did, the van was still there, Greg leaning against the side, a curl of smoke rising from a lit joint in his hand.

***

I found a small B&B in a cul-de-sac just off the main street. It looked like a family home; through the drawn-back curtains I could see a family clustered around the living-room table, just clearing away the remains of a meal. I checked the sign again to make sure I had the right house, then pressed my thumb to the doorbell. The woman who answered the door a few moments later seemed taken aback at the sight of my rucksack.

'Yes, we've got a room free,' she said uncertainly, her soft Scottish accent sounding welcoming but reserved. 'We're no doing meals at this time of year, I'm afraid. Just the bed part of the bed and breakfast.'

'That's OK. I've got a dehydrated meal in my pack. All I need is a kettle.'

'That I can do,' the woman said with a smile, and led me inside.

I had to stoop to fit under the doorframe with my pack on. The heat from the hall hit me like an oven and I felt myself sweating within seconds. I'd become fully acclimatised to the outdoor life in late February in Scotland – not cold for the time of year, but a lot cooler than this family's central heating.

'Say hello,' the woman said brightly as we passed the open door leading into the front room. A balding middle-aged man in a chunky knitted sweater creased into a smile and raised a hand, and a teenage lad looked up from his phone with an awkward expression, self-conscious but not unfriendly, that told me he had been asked to greet a thousand guests before.

The room was small, clean, basic, and perfect in every way. After checking myself and my gear thoroughly in the bathroom for ticks, and rinsing myself down in a scaldingly hot shower, I returned to my room and passed out on the bed.

***

Day 24: 1 March 2019

As I walked through the deserted streets of the village early the next morning, I sensed that the weather was starting to change. High-tailed cirrus streaked in elongated commas across a sky of blue so pale as to be almost white, and this monochrome texture looked inviting enough to reach up and touch. All of that springtime sap-rising energy had drained suddenly out of the atmosphere. If my previous week on the Cape Wrath Trail had been more winter–spring than winter, now I felt the invisible compass turning again, signalling that it wasn't all over quite yet. The snow and high winds could return again at any time. Maybe it was a good thing that I was nearing the end, that I'd be at Cape Wrath in two days.

At the SPAR general store next to the harbour, I left my pack and poles on the concrete step outside and trundled around the narrow aisles, grabbing more items than I needed and dropping them into the shopping basket. I left the store with more than enough food to last me until I got to the Cape and back to Durness. Back outside, I found my way to the picnic area behind the industrial estate, overlooking a beach, and ate an entire Selkirk bannock then and there while I fished my gear out of my bag and shook it all down again, hoping to dislodge any remaining ticks. I wasn't surprised when I found a few stowaways lurking in the deepest folds of my sleeping bag. What surprised me was that none had bitten me.

Packed again and ready to go, I began the walk out of Kinlochbervie and along the shore road towards Oldshoremore and Sheigra. Little stirred. There was a single ship in the harbour, a massive rust-streaked vessel chained to the dock, and a few containers and pallets of goods stood here and there on the hard standing. I quickly turned left and climbed the hill, passing a van parked in a layby.

The van looked familiar.

As I walked past it, I recognised the dull green paintwork and grimy windows of the van that had given me a lift into the village last night. Greg's van. There was a curtain pulled across the windscreen but I found myself speeding up, hoping that I wouldn't be spotted, that he'd keep snoring in his bunk until I was well away from the road and on the trail to Sandwood Bay. As I continued along the undulating single-track road between wire fences and open moorland, past a ruined house made from not much more than a few sheets of white-painted corrugated iron held together by seams of rust, I tried to remember what I'd told Greg. Had I told him where I was going, where I planned to stay? I didn't think so. *Stop worrying*, I told myself. *He isn't lying in wait for you. He probably decided it was too late to go looking for a campsite at the beach and decided to kip in the layby instead. Just keep walking. In a few kilometres you'll be off the road and completely safe.*

My brain struggled to process the nature of this threat. I'd often been frightened while hiking, or while high in the mountains, but always the threats had been tangible, easy to understand: lightning at altitude, rockfall, the risk of falling. This was unknowable and amorphous. It felt more like anxiety itself. Suddenly I realised that I'd been privileged to have never felt unsafe in this particular way before.

After less than half an hour, I heard a whining fan belt and chugging engine coming up the hill behind me. I didn't look back, but I knew that it would be Greg's van. It was the only vehicle I'd seen since hitting the road again at Rhiconich the afternoon before. The van screeched to a halt beside me and Greg wound down his window with that laborious squeaking noise.

'All right, mate?'

'Hi,' I said.

He was wearing the same clothes I'd seen him in last night, with the addition of a pair of dark glasses pushed up on to his forehead beneath the brim of his flat cap. He rested one hand against the steering wheel and tapped it lightly as we spoke, as if grooving to an unheard rhythm.

'Find any ticks in your gear last night? Your name was mud last night after I'd dropped you off.'

He sounded amused rather than angry, but I guessed that if I told him the truth then his good humour might turn. 'No, everything was clear. Ticks don't seem to like me much.'

'Thank fuck for that. Name's Greg, by the way.' He reached a hand out of the window for me to shake, and I did so. This time I noticed that he wore a paracord bracelet around his wrist, and another wristband behind it saying something about archery.

I decided not to remind him that he'd already introduced himself last night. Then I wondered if he had done this deliberately, to keep me standing here in the middle of the road talking for a few minutes longer. The van's engine was still ticking over. Nobody would walk away just after an introduction, would they? Despite my mounting unease, I almost laughed – it was too ridiculously British.

Perhaps sensing my thoughts, he suddenly grinned. 'Bet you were scared last night when you saw my weapons in the back, eh? Big archery fan. Truck driver by trade, but should have been in the forces. Medical. You know how it is.'

'Oh.'

'Me dad were in the Paras.'

He seemed to expect a response. I nodded, but decided that it was time to move on. 'Look, it's been nice chatting again, but I've got to get walking. Got a lot more miles to do today.' I forced a smile. 'Reckon the weather's going to turn later.'

I raised a hand and turned away. The van's brakes gave out a squeal and the vehicle kept pace with me as I walked. I realised that there wasn't a lot I could do to get away from him if he was determined to talk to me, so I stopped.

'Where are you heading tonight, then?' Greg said cheerily.

'I don't know yet. I might camp. There are a couple of bothies.'

'You get some right weirdos in bothies. I prefer camping. Bit of a bush-craft fan myself.' He was eyeing up my rucksack again. 'I bet all that gear cost a fortune. How do you afford it? Are you a dentist or summat?'

At this point my threat detector was hovering somewhere between 'mostly harmless' and 'weird situation but not imminently lethal'. Greg had decided that this conversation was going to happen, and I couldn't do anything about it.

'I'm an outdoor writer,' I said, leaning forward against my trekking poles to take some of my pack's weight off my back. 'I'm doing this trip as a commission for a magazine. Part of the job involves testing new kit. It's been supplied by the brands.'

Greg's eyebrows shot up. 'And you do this for a fucking living? Walking hundreds of miles in winter? Hope they're paying you well.' He reached out and felt the fabric of my waterproof jacket between a finger and thumb, and I reflexively moved back. 'Feels flimsy to me. I wouldn't trust it in severe weather. You'd be better off with Ventile.'

Ventile is an ancient cotton-based fabric, first used in waterproof clothing during the Second World War. Its mainstream use had died out long ago thanks to the advent of lightweight breathable membranes such as Gore-Tex. I had no idea that anyone still used it on the hill.

'Right,' I said.

'I've got a custom-made Ventile smock. Dog's proverbials. Give me a sec ... '

Greg twisted around to rummage in the passenger footwell, and after a moment – 'Aha!' – he triumphantly held the garment out of the window for me to have a look at. I dutifully peered at it. The fabric was the same musty shade of green as his van, plus a few coffee or gravy stains. With a tone of pride, Greg explained its features in great detail, pointed out the various pockets within pockets he'd added to the design. 'It'll wet out after a few hours,' he admitted, 'but if it's raining that hard just pitch your tent and wait it out, see?'

'That's incredible,' I said, and meant it.

He looked pleased. 'I tell you what, mate, you write for the outdoor magazines, you should review one of these Ventile coats. Let me write down the make.' He reached forward to sift through the junk on his dashboard and fished out a Post-it note pad, then wrote the name of the brand in blocky capitals with the stub of a pencil. After the briefest pause, he glanced at me and then wrote 'GREG' at the bottom, followed by his phone number.

'In case you want me to put you in touch with them,' he said. 'You could pass a jacket like this down to your kids, if you ever get married.'

I distinctly remembered mentioning my wife last night, and I wondered again if he was leading the conversation in a deliberate way. Or maybe he was just forgetful. 'I'm already married, actually,' I said.

'Oh, right.' He looked at me for a moment. 'In case you want to chat about gear, then, maybe. Look, I don't expect we'll be best buddies or owt like that, but I'd be keen to know how you get on after your exped, like. I know what you're thinking, he's just a sad old geezer who likes young men, but I find it int'lectually stimulating talking to like-minded individuals.'

I sensed truth in what he was saying, and I nodded, but I was still acutely aware that I hadn't seen a single other car yet that day, and there wasn't a house in sight either way along the road. I'd decided that he was probably harmless after all, but that background hum of unease hadn't gone away entirely.

'Are you on WhatsApp?' he added.

I'd started to walk again, and the van trundled along beside me at walking pace, Greg leaning out of the window as he kept one hand on the wheel.

'No, I don't like Facebook as a rule,' I said.

'Very wise, mate. Very wise. I deleted my Facebook and Instagram accounts – only use WhatsApp because it's encrypted. Mind you, fuck knows who's listening, eh?'

'More people should be sceptical of these platforms,' I said, just to fill the expectant pause, but by the way his eyes lit up I could tell I'd pushed a button. I wished I'd just smiled and nodded and walked a bit faster.

'Too right. These platforms are the tools of the paedophile liberal elite. Mate, you owe it to yourself to get educated. We are just cattle to be slaughtered by our reptilian overlords, and that's the truth of it.'

OK, what?

While I stood there like a deer frozen in headlights, unable to look away, he embarked upon an epic fifteen-minute rant about his grand unifying theory of everything wrong with the world – and it included most of the conspiracy theories I'd ever heard of. It was dazzling in its magnificence, but it wasn't a conversation. It was a lecture. YouTube was, it turned out, his primary source of information, alongside books by someone called Immanuel Velikovsky.

' … and *that's* why mercury poisoning in the flu vaccine is all about thinning the human herd and concentrating power in the hands of the Venus-worshipping cultists. There will be a global pandemic either this year or next, you'll see. Surprised you've never heard of the HAARP superweapon, to be honest.' He paused for breath, then sniffed. 'Don't even get me started on so-called global warming.' He waited for me to get him started, then got started anyway. 'It's a hoax, all made up for scientists to get rich. As is the idea of the Ice Age.'

'Really?'

'Them glacial erratics they're always talking about? Put there by glaciers? Bollocks. They were deposited there by global super-tsunamis caused by the gravitational collapse of Planet X ten million years ago.' He nodded. 'Which was of course planned. And that leads me on to Brexit—'

That was the final straw for me. 'Look, I really must get going,' I said as firmly as I could. 'I've got a long way to walk today.'

Greg looked awkward, almost shy. 'Right, right. Yeah, sorry to keep you. It's just nice to find someone who'll listen, eh? Someone who reads. Let me recommend you these books. They'll open your eyes, mate.' He produced another Post-it note and carefully inscribed 'IMMANULLE VALLIKOVSKEE WORLDS-IN-COLLINSION + EARTH-IN-UP-HEVAL'. I took the scrap of paper and put it in my pocket.

'I'm on my way down south now, promise,' he said with a grin. 'Hope the rest of the exped goes well.'

With that, he wound his window back up again, and I heard the van reverse into a three-point turn before speeding back down the lane towards Kinlochbervie. I walked on.

Two minutes later, I burst into a fit of laughter that had me gasping.

***

As I left the road and began walking the path towards the dunes of Sandwood Bay, I couldn't help thinking about Greg – about solitude, about connection and disconnection, and about the way these things had warped and turned inwards to forge a lonely and disappointed and credulous soul, so desperate for meaning that he latched on to every story that came along until his heart was full of them. I knew that algorithmic content feeds such as YouTube had the power to radicalise people and entrench worldviews, make moderate beliefs more extreme with every recommended video and every like. Anti-vaxxers, political extremism, 5G conspiracy theories, even the rise of Donald Trump: I believed that all of these things had been intensified or enhanced by the internet, that great engine of confirmation bias and acceleration burning through our world.

Was Greg walking, talking proof that I'd been right about the internet all along – that it was a malign force? Or, I suddenly realised, had the same process of algorithmic bias sent my own opinions and beliefs into a black hole as I researched the negative effects of social media? Maybe I had been radicalised too, in a way. Given enough time on my own, enough web searches for 'how to block Twitter', would I end up like Greg?

Is this what I sound like to Hannah when I moan about Facebook and Google and how they invade our privacy? Is this what I sound like to our friends when I rant about why I won't install so-called Internet of Things tech in our house?

Maybe there was something in that, but after so long out on the trail I could hardly even put myself back into that frame of mind any more. I could no longer bring myself to care that much. They seemed like the anxieties of another person living another life.

Ahead lay Sandwood Bay. The beginning of the end.

PART 5
Furtherance

Chapter 14

As a child, I was obsessed by fantasy novels. The works of J.R.R. Tolkien and Ursula Le Guin helped to shape a view of the world in which ordinary places had a tangible magic, if you just knew how to look; and although adulthood had dulled that spark it hadn't put it out altogether. I liked to think that the Cape Wrath Trail had brought just a bit of it back, that maybe I'd remembered something of that more innocent way of seeing.

Ursula Le Guin's *Earthsea* novels left a particularly strong imprint. The hero, Ged, was a wanderer and a seeker of solitude, one who sought to be quiet and listen to the world. I identified with that. The tale that made the greatest impression on me was book 3, *The Farthest Shore* – a story of a strange sickness creeping across the lands, causing magic to lose its power, people to lose hope, life itself to wilt and die. As the heroes sought to find the source of this evil (which turned out to be a wizard named Cob), they eventually came to the beach of Selidor, the outermost island facing the infinite ocean, where they found the bones of a dragon rising up from the sand. Of such potent symbols are citadels of childhood imagination built. And they can echo down the years, causing strange ripples in our adult lives.

Sometimes on my journey north to Cape Wrath I'd felt like Bilbo Baggins in *The Hobbit,* off on a mildly perilous but ultimately jolly quest into the wild (minus the Elvish singing). Sometimes I'd just felt like a bloke wandering about in soggy countryside for no very good reason. Sometimes, especially as I drew close to Sandwood Bay, I felt like Ged, storm-lashed and adrift, seeking to learn more about the source of my anxiety so that I might vanquish it from the world. I'd already come so far, and I knew that I was close.

Just like on my first Cape Wrath Trail, I met no one on the footpath from Blairmore, past the eerie silver waters of Loch na Gainimh, and over the hills towards the smell of the sea. I passed between a pair of ancient lichen-furred posts that seemed to signify a gateway. Beyond, I saw the wide expanse of a greater body of water – Sandwood Loch – and beyond that, the brown hills and receding horizon of Cape Wrath itself.

The roll and crash of breakers reached my ears.

***

If the Cape Wrath Trail is a journey of stepping from one world into the next, then Sandwood Bay marks the last (and the most magnificent) of these boundaries, a place wreathed in mystique and trail lore. For many, a wild camp on the beach, or huddled amongst the labyrinth of dunes, is a rite of passage – one as essential to the CWT experience as passing under Glenfinnan Viaduct or a selfie at the lighthouse. Sandwood Bay appears on its fair share of 'Top ten best beaches in Scotland' lists, and for good reason. A pristine sweep of white sand over a mile long, facing out into the Atlantic, it can be a place either of warm sunshine or of unimaginable ferocity. The picture-postcard and the raw sublime meet in the middle here to create an unstable world that is never quite one thing or the other. To the west, the rock monolith of Am Buachaille juts out of the surf: a finger pointing in judgement at the heavens. Even on a benign day in June, when there are a dozen picnic rugs spread on the beach and laughing children playing in the dunes, that uneasy sense of the sublime is never far away.

To be alone in such a place is to commune directly with nature at the edge of the world – that's what a Romantic-era poet would say, anyway. For the people of Kinlochbervie, Oldshoremore, Blairmore and Sheigra, it's a pleasant spot for picnics and dog walking. I didn't know what I would find at my own farthest shore when I got there, but due to the fact that it was early March in the far north-west of Scotland I certainly expected to be alone.

I descended through marram grass to the beach, walking on damp sand beneath a sky that had dulled as the day had matured. A chilly breeze made me zip up the collar of my coat and put my gloves back on. Ahead, the sea breathed in and out, and I saw that golden smile of sand at the edge of it, stretching in a leisurely arc out towards the sea cliffs of Cape Wrath. I already knew I wouldn't be camping here, though; I wanted to make for the bothy at Strathchailleach a few miles further on. Not only would that give me a head start on the final day to the Cape, it would also put a bit more space between me and Greg, should he change his mind about heading south and decide to come looking for me after all. I didn't think that was likely, but once the idea came to me I couldn't dislodge it.

The beach invited me to walk along it, to leave the official line of the path behind and stroll closer to the surf. Towards the end of the beach, where the outflow from Sandwood Loch formed a river that had to be forded, I saw a monolithic object rising up in front of me like a land-bound echo of Am Buachaille. The slender object pointed up out of the sand at an angle. For a while as I walked towards it my brain failed to make any sense of what I was seeing. Was it a standing stone? I didn't remember one being here. A colossal piece of driftwood, perhaps?

As I drew closer, its form coalesced. It was a skull of gargantuan proportions protruding at least four feet from where it grew out of the sand. I saw the dark hollows of eye sockets and a tapered snout that looked like the tine of a sundial. My mind grappled with words to describe what I was seeing, and all I could come up with were *dinosaur* and *dragon*.

At last I stood before it, filled with a sense of profound reverence and mystery.

The surface looked weathered, salt-corroded, ground down by the action of sand and pebbles. Sand filled every crevice and hollow. It looked more like a fossil or an extrusion of the world itself than the relic of a living creature. I wondered how long it had been there.

All I could think of was that story from my childhood, of Ged coming at last to the farthest shore of Selidor and finding the bones of the dragon on the beach. It was a place of confrontation between Ged, the hero, and Cob, the evil sorcerer – and although Ged didn't succeed in vanquishing

Cob on Selidor, that beach at the edge of everything was a turning point in the quest. A tipping over from darkness to light.

As I stared at the skull before me, another word floated up to the conscious levels of my mind. *Whale.* This was no dragon, but a whale skull, and as such it had far greater significance.

I knew little about cetaceans – just enough to be well aware that whales, dolphins and porpoises were facing catastrophe in British waters.[1] An increasing number of whales were getting beached. This usually resulted in the death of the animal. My brother had told me that there were many possible causes of whale strandings, including pollutants, ship strikes, noise pollution and disease. Indirect human interference was usually the common factor. More precisely, whale strandings were a symptom of a much bigger malaise affecting almost everything on the planet: the twin catastrophes of biodiversity loss and climate change. Like Cob's dark magic casting a numbing grey shroud over Earthsea.

This was not the first sign of these looming disasters I'd seen on my journey to Cape Wrath. I'd walked through a landscape of ghost forests and plundered natural wealth, of biodiversity islands clinging to life. I'd walked through a disappearing winter. I'd camped on a tick nest in February and sweated in unseasonal heat. Although the plural of anecdote is not data, and nothing I'd seen was hard evidence of a warming and dying world, everything within me screamed that these things meant something. That what I had witnessed mattered.

Now I stood face to face with a totem of the death our species was bringing – a death vast in scale and seemingly impossible to disentangle, made all the worse by the fact that we were doing it unintentionally. Most of us don't get up in the morning and think *looking forward to another day of plundering the earth's resources.* We just consume, and we breed, and we dispose of our rubbish, and a little more of the world dies.

Almost as an afterthought, I remembered the anxieties that had pro-

---

1 A report on whale and dolphin strandings published in September 2019 concluded that there had been 4,896 reports of stranded cetaceans in the UK between January 2011 and December 2017 – a fifteen per cent increase on the previous period. Many of the incidents involved numerous animals, including mass strandings of pilot whales.

pelled me to make this journey in the first place: overwhelm, the cease-less noise of the internet, chronic distraction, and a desperate yearning to experience genuine, unmediated solitude. Well, I'd had my fill of solitude now, enough to realise that I had both romanticised it and expected too much from it. One of the lessons this trail had taught me was that my anxiety did not stem from the internet or anything in it, but was simply part of who I was, and could be triggered by many things. I'd missed the internet as much as I'd relished being away from it. I'd craved connection as much as disconnection. I no longer even recognised the state of mind I'd been spiralling towards before the start of the trail. I thought about what Seb had told me back at the Forest Way Bunkhouse: that it was easy to look for a convenient external cause when the more difficult questions were within.

This, right here, was what mattered: a rotting whale skull on a beach in Scotland on the edge of a snowless winter. The gravity of this place seemed to bend the fabric of reality around it, and I'd already seen enough for it to wipe all thoughts of internet anxiety from my mind. Like a victim of the Total Perspective Vortex in *The Hitchhiker's Guide to the Galaxy* (another favourite childhood read), I found myself reeling as I stood there, stupefied by the new idea that gripped me.

You've been worrying about the wrong things. The decline of wildlife in the wild places you love is far more important. Our rapidly changing climate is far more important.

Anxiety would never be far away, I knew that now, but I could choose what I focused on, what I noticed. At that moment, standing before the dragon, I pledged to notice the things that mattered.

***

There are some sections of the Cape Wrath Trail that feel inevitable. The landscape of this bleak and almost entirely uninhabited peninsula is un-compromising in every way: a range of low, boggy mountains, bounded by unbroken sea cliffs to the west and north and an estuary to the east. Only from the south is it easily accessible on foot. Like many other parts of the Highlands, it supported many small crofting communities until the people were cleared and their land given over to the sheep. The Ministry of Defence owns a fair chunk of the peninsula – fifty-nine square kilometres devoted to military training, including a naval gunnery range. The small island of An Garbh-eilean is the main target for ordnance, and it regularly gets 1,000-pound bombs flung at it. On my first visit I had seen craters from stray bombs that had landed near the road leading through the area to the lighthouse. It was a place of big skies, big silences and a sense of quiet, still freedom – except during military exercises, when access to the northern half was restricted and red flags flew along the barbed-wire fence marking the perimeter of the MoD land.

With access to MoD land restricted during military exercises, including the lighthouse at the end of the trail, it was vital to find out whether an exercise would be running *before* leaving Kinlochbervie (the last place with any reliable phone signal). Back in 2015, I'd tried to call range control for an update, but hadn't been able to get through and decided to press on anyway. When I reached the access road to the lighthouse, a sentry found me, asked me to get into his waiting Land Rover and cordially informed me that the RAF would be starting their bombardment in ten minutes. He drove me to the lighthouse and we had a chat about walking, seabirds, and just how much of a bang a 1,000-pound bomb makes when it misses its target and explodes on the mainland by accident. 'That's why we always ask walkers to check before crossing the fence,' he said. 'We respect your access rights, but we can't keep you safe during exercises.'

I took the point. This time, when I rang range control from the picnic bench outside the SPAR in the village, I got through on the first try. The person on the other end of the phone told me that no exercises would be taking place for weeks. Green light.

The fact that Cape Wrath was an active bombing run, and could only be accessed by hopping over a barbed-wire fence in between bombardments, added a little extra spice to the adventure.

The danger area begins several kilometres to the north-east of Sandwood Bay, along the line of the Keisgaig River. Crossing the boundary fence would be a job for the final day. I had decided to spend the night at the remote bothy of Strathchailleach, a place with a rich and interesting history all of its own. It could also claim to be one of the most isolated bothies in Scotland. No path led to it, or led away from it; north of Sandwood Bay, the Cape Wrath Trail plunged into trackless moorland, a maze of compass bearings and bogs and contour lines, and did not find a track again of any kind until it reached the final few kilometres of road to the lighthouse. A fitting end to a big walk in the wild.

The low-roofed cottage came into view as I contoured around a hill covered in boulders of a striking variegated pattern. The terrain was rougher than I remembered, but the flat ground down there beside the river looked like uniform bog. I descended to the bothy. Although I'd expected to be sloshing through pools between the tufts of rushes and tussocks of grass, the ground was firm and almost dry. I remembered that it had barely rained for a long time.

Strathchailleach made a statement with its crayon-red door and low, shallow roof with a chimney and peat store at one end. It was squatter than the average bothy, flattened to the ground like a hare in a stubble field or a dwarf birch bent over by the wind on some freezing northern tundra. The building was of the place. It too felt inevitable.

The door creaked open at my touch and I stepped inside gingerly, wondering if I would be alone. An exploration of the various rooms and cubbyholes revealed no one. I let myself relax, and marvelled at the remarkable paintings and murals that could still be seen on some of the walls.

This house was occupied by James 'Sandy' McRory Smith, a hermit, for thirty-two years. He lived in the cottage from the winter of 1962, by which point the building had already been vacant for at least a decade. McRory Smith made the abandoned building his home, and it's thought that Strathchailleach was the last permanently inhabited dwelling in the UK with no services whatsoever: no electricity, no running water, no gas, no road access. He liked it that way. Contemporary accounts often described him as cantankerous and eccentric, although he could be generous to visitors as often as he was hostile. In 1979 the cottage suffered storm damage and McRory Smith had to move out. The Mountain Bothies Association, who had wanted to take on the building for some time, took his absence as an opportunity, and by the following year repairs were well underway. By 1981, McRory Smith was back on the scene and wanted the cottage back. He struck a deal with the MBA: they'd get to open Strathchailleach as a bothy for hillwalkers and backpackers, but only if McRory Smith could move back in as before.

It didn't work. Conflicts arose between McRory Smith and bothy visitors. By 1984 Strathchailleach was no longer listed as a bothy and the inhabitant got what he wanted once again: uninterrupted solitude. But he moved out for the last time in 1994 due to ill health, and the building has been maintained as a bothy ever since.

The last permanent inhabitant of Strathchailleach died in 1999. He left a complicated legacy. To some he is remembered with bitterness, as someone who took advantage of the MBA and failed to uphold his side of the bargain. To others he's a hero and a symbol of solitude, like Christopher McCandless alone in the Magic Bus in the middle of the Alaskan wilderness. People who choose to live out their lives in such isolation – who fight for it with everything they have and are never happy or fulfilled in what we call the real world – fascinate us in life and often become icons after death.

I looked up at the framed portrait of McRory Smith mounted on the wall above a shelf of damp and curling paperbacks. His deeply lined face, set within a halo of white beard and a green woolly hat, stared out of the picture with an expression that demanded what the hell the viewer was looking at.

As I traced my fingers over the murals Sandy had left behind on the walls of the old cottage, the painted colours fading but still vibrant, I thought about the simple life he must have led here. Wind, rain, sunshine, cutting and drying peat, making do, walking miles to the post office to collect his pension and purchase supplies, the pungent smell of tobacco and peat smoke, the never-ending music of the river. Peace. And yet life here must have been hard. Had solitude ever collapsed into loneliness? Did boredom dull the beauty of Cape Wrath from time to time? Did anxiety or depression stalk him?

Sandy's paintings depicted simple scenes: a pony against a hillside, a woman carrying a baby, a woman with a harp. I imagined him creating the pictures in the light streaming through rain-washed windows, then making the finishing touches by the wavering glow of a Tilley lantern. Had he been moved to create them by some unstoppable artistic urge, or had he just been bored out of his mind and wanted something to do? Even as I asked myself this question I knew that I probably wouldn't understand the answer. Perhaps he didn't need a reason. Perhaps just being here in this place, and finding a way to express himself, was enough.

Later, after I'd made my bed in the small back room and gathered dry peat from the lean-to peat store outside, then gone and cut more peat from the bank to replace the sods I'd taken, I relaxed in an old camp chair someone had left for bothy visitors. I'd hung my socks on the plastic coat hangers dangling on the washing line over the fireplace. I'd checked the bothy book – no entry from my friend Skye – and prodded at the strange collection of objects on the shelf, which included a box of Tesco blister plasters that expired in March 2017, a spray bottle of Smidge, a small torch with dead batteries, and innumerable dead flies.

The fire, when I finally managed to light the not-quite-dry-enough peat, smelled like a mouthful of cask-strength Laphroaig. I breathed in as much of it as I could. My socks were getting thoroughly marinated in the smoke up there on the washing line. I couldn't take this glorious smell back into the real world, but perhaps the memory of it would help to keep this reality from fading for just a while longer.

***

Day 25: 2 March 2019

'One day more … '

The song came to me unbidden as I left Strathchailleach the next morning. I had not slept well. Rain had hammered on the bothy roof for hours, and it took me an unusually long time to drift off. As I lay there in my sleeping bag I wondered again if Greg might change his mind and come looking for me after all. He didn't, of course. The bothy door stayed shut, my solitude disturbed by no one but the mice.

The river had risen by an inch or two overnight. I picked my way across the stepping stones that Sandy McRory Smith must have crossed a thousand times or more on his way to the place where the finest peat in Scotland could be cut from a low bank, or so it was reputed. Onward. The sun shone fierce out of a cloudless sky. I'd geared myself up for a battle against the weather. While yesterday had felt Cape Wrathy in every possible sense, today I felt dislodged from the experience I'd expected, like the soundtrack of a movie not quite in sync with the picture. Perhaps there was a lesson there. Experience does not always bend to expectations.

I began the bleak cross-country moorland stomp to the lighthouse. The terrain was wet and boggy, but not excessively so, and I found myself appreciating the amazing variety of textures and colours at my feet: the porous, branching pale green of reindeer moss; grey pillows of densely packed, drier mosses; the yellows and burnt oranges of many different species of grass; the surprising skeletal white structures of exposed heather stalks.

I took a wandering line, following only vaguely the course I'd plotted on my GPS. When I reached Loch Keisgaig, I was relieved to see no red flag flying at the boundary, which was a simple barbed-wire fence, easy to hop over. I crossed at a faded signpost that said 'Military Firing Range. Keep out when red flags are flying or red lamps are lit'. On the other side, in the military zone, the landscape looked identical: a vast rolling duvet of peat and moss and grass and bog.

***

The land was running out beneath my boots. Soon there would be no more north. Soon my lighthouse-to-lighthouse journey would be complete.

It was a strange feeling, coming down from the range of low hills on the north of the peninsula and seeing the land narrowing to a point before me, and nothing but the inverted V of the Atlantic beyond.

The lighthouse on the farthest point was hidden from sight behind one final hill and would remain so until the last few hundred metres to the end of the trail. Although I could make out the slender thread of the road weaving from east to west along the edge of the cliffs – a lifeline between the isolated community of Cape Wrath and the nearest village of Durness, on the mainland – its touch was light in this elemental place. I could see no evidence whatsoever that this was part of a military testing zone. Water, ground, moss, rock, air, and bright the seagull's flight on the empty sky (to paraphrase Ursula Le Guin). 'Only in silence the word,' she had written; 'only in dark the light'.

Of silence I had drunk deeply. Deep enough to realise that there is no silence, that there are no blank canvasses, that no landscape is empty.

The lighthouse came into view at last from the gravel track curving around the headland towards the clifftops. A white monolith jutting above a gaunt clutch of outbuildings, some ruined, it stood at the edge of everything (well, the British mainland) and seemed to lend a grim finality to the last stage of my walk. 'This far you can walk,' it seemed to say, 'but no further. On the plus side, we have cake.' At that point, I was looking forward to coffee and baked goods at the Ozone Café more than finishing my walk.

Ten more minutes were all it took. As I approached the compound along the final curve of the road, I saw a woman with a dog high on the hillside to my right, and at the sight of me she started back towards the lighthouse at a brisk pace. I strolled into the yard a few minutes after her, passing several Land Rovers and a rusting van, then a huge oil tank on a concrete plinth huddled all around by the squat whitewashed buildings. Some had been reclaimed; others had the grimed and greening look of buildings well on their way to becoming ruins.

The twin red doors to the Ozone Café stood ajar. I dumped my pack outside and walked a few more metres to the low wall surrounding the lighthouse. The monolith rose up in front of me: fresh white banded with a few concentric sand-yellow rings, and narrow slots of windows leading the eye up to the crystalline black glass of the light itself at the top. That was it. No surge of emotion, no feeling of accomplishment.

On autopilot, I fished my satellite tracker out of its pocket, turned it on, and pressed the check-in button.

Time for some food.

***

The shutter above the counter clattered up as I entered the café, and a woman in a fluffy jumper waved at me with a smile. The room was cold. It was the sort of room that's difficult to keep warm at the best of times – high ceiling, tiled floor, big windows, brick walls – but I quickly formed the impression that I was the first customer to have come along for ages, and that they hadn't been using the heating. I didn't mind. The chilly temperature felt comfortable to me now.

I approached the counter, and the woman smiled again at me. She was stroking a large black-and-white cat that sat in the crook of her arm, purring contentedly. Last time I'd been to Cape Wrath I'd met John Ure, the enterprising man who had built a business in this isolated corner of Scotland – isolated in winter, at least, but surprisingly busy with mini-bus-loads of tourists in the summer season. This must be his daughter, Angela.

'I wasn't sure you'd be open at this time of year,' I said to her.

'Oh, we always open if we see a hiker. I saw you from up on the hill.' She paused. 'We've got lentil soup. Or I could make you a cooked break-fast.'

I asked for the latter. While she got the stove going and brewed me a pot of coffee, I asked her if she'd seen Skye: 'Sixteen-year-old lad, hiking Land's End to John o'Groats.'

'No, you're the first CWT hiker we've seen in weeks,' she called from the kitchen. 'Not many do it in winter. There was a couple a few weeks ago.'

That could only mean that Skye was still behind me – or that he'd got off the trail. I had a strong feeling that he had decided to follow my advice and take it easy for a few days, and that he'd be along to complete the CWT when the time was right for him.

Angela brought over a huge pot of coffee and a cup and saucer. She smiled at me again – the gentle, patient smile of someone at home in their own company.

'Thank you,' I said. 'Can I ask you something? What's it like living out here? Does it get lonely?'

She looked surprised, and paused for a moment to consider her answer. 'Well, I suppose it does sometimes,' she said unhurriedly. 'But it's nice too. Time seems to run at its proper pace, I think.'

I thought I knew what she meant. 'And would you say the Cape Wrath Trail is becoming more popular?'

'It's my first season out here helping my dad, but I'd say yes. It comes in fits and starts, though. Dad tells me things got busier about three or four years ago. It's been good, actually,' she added. 'More customers have helped the business to grow. If nobody wanted to come here then the lighthouse would rot and no one would see all this beauty.'

Breakfast was a gigantic plate of bacon, fried eggs, black pudding, beans, toast, and another half-litre of coffee. I thumbed through the visitors' book as I ate. Its pages had that slightly damp, slightly grimy feeling of paper left in a bothy or a shed, or pages handled by many grubby hands. The visitors' book was incomplete – Angela told me that she often forgot to mention it to Cape Wrath Trail completers, and a new one for 2019 had not yet been started.

'Where are you stopping tonight?' Angela asked me when I deposited my empty plate back on the counter and thanked her for the meal.

'Kearvaig bothy,' I said.

A kind of wonder bloomed over her features. 'Oh, Kearvaig is lovely. Magical. You'll know when you get there.'

Chapter 15

The neat narrative I'd been building in my head, of Sandwood Bay as the farthest shore and everything on the other side as some metaphorical calmer sea beyond it, fell apart as I trudged down the track to Kearvaig Bay in driving wind and rain. I could hardly feel my fingers through my thin liner gloves. This felt more like winter at last. I had passed beyond another invisible threshold – and this was one I could never re-cross. The trail had come to an end, and now everything felt different. By the time I descended the track to this isolated haven, the white cottage and its golden beach surrounded by sea cliffs and flying salt spray, I was completely soaked.

Kearvaig is the northernmost bothy in the UK, facing north with no land between its secluded bay (one of the only safe landings on Cape Wrath) and the Arctic. For many Cape Wrath Trail hikers, it has become the traditional place to spend the final night on the trail before the walk out to Durness. Angela had been right – there was intangible magic here.

The cottage wore a soft sheep-cropped lawn around itself like a blanket. You could pitch fifty tents here – a hundred. I imagined what this place must be like when MBA volunteers congregated for a big work party. It was silent as I approached. Even as I walked the last few metres to the rear door I knew that I would find it empty, as I had found almost every bothy on the Cape Wrath Trail empty. Four months from now this place would feel very different.

Unusually for bothies in Scotland, this one was divided into two completely distinct buildings with no way of getting from one to the other without going back outside. The rear door led to a small, cosy room with a fireplace, table, bookshelves, and a few sleeping platforms. The door at the other end of the building opened up to a miniature palace with several downstairs rooms and a massive upper storey. The aesthetic was bright, with white-painted walls and smart varnished wood: a tidy bothy kept in good order by its maintenance volunteers. I imagined that thirty or forty people could comfortably sleep within Kearvaig's walls.

After taking my time exploring the nooks and crannies of the bigger half, laughing out loud at the hand-scrawled Kearvaig Bothy Code poster someone had Blu-Tacked to the wall, I returned to the smaller back room and made myself at home.[1]

***

It was coming to an end now. I knew that. By this time tomorrow I'd be in a hostel in Durness and my phone would be connected to the internet again and all the clutter and complexity of the world out there would be back in here, back in my head. The simplicity and the stillness would be gone – or maybe not gone, but changed from a lived truth to a memory half preserved and half pressed out of shape by the weight of the world. Time would speed up and run away from me. I knew that no matter how many photos I took, how many words I wrote in my journal, I could never capture exactly what I had felt and done and who I had been. The essence of experience cannot be recorded. These moments would be gone. Such is the pathos of being human, but at that moment I felt the echo of that future loss keenly.

I lit candles not against the dark, but to welcome it in. The meagre store of driftwood and old fence posts some previous visitor had stacked left of the fireplace occupied me for half an hour as I chopped with a blunt axe. Later, the wood fuelled a reluctant and smoky fire. In front of the fireplace there was a chair – more like a throne, really – constructed out of bits of

---

1 The poster consisted of a long list, including: 'No shoes to be worn in this bothy. No beards in this bothy. No farting in this bothy. No cooking or eating in this bothy. No potholing in this bothy. No combine harvesting in this bothy. No jousting in this bothy. No prospecting for uranium in this bothy.'

flotsam and jetsam. It had a stocky, heavy look, and it cradled the sitter close to the floor. Someone had scrawled 'KING OF KEARVAIG' on one of the rough planks. I eased myself down into the throne and sat there with my legs stretched out towards the blaze, watching the steam rise from my damp trousers and bare feet.

Slotted in between several books on the shelf by the window I found the bothy book. It covered 2013 to the present day, and I thumbed back to read my own entry from 22 June 2015, when I had completed my first Cape Wrath Trail. Leafing further back, I was interested to find an entry by Will Copestake, written on 6 August 2013:

Arrived late by sea kayak which I'm taking solo around Scotland and climbing all 282 Munros. What a fantastic 5* bothy!

Next to this entry, a note:

Well done, Will! ☺ *Al Humphreys, 2015*

Amongst all the other entries, these from well-known outdoor person-alities leapt out at me. I'd interacted with both online but didn't know them personally. I was accustomed to thinking of them as professional adventurers – people who had managed to carve out a living from writing books and doing talks and outdoor guiding, and who therefore had to convert their outdoor experiences into products. I was on that spectrum too, but not as far along. Did professional adventurers ever regret the choice to go pro? Did they ever long for a simpler time when they didn't have to film their trips or write about them?

Such questions had long absorbed me as an outdoor writer, but in this time capsule I saw hope burning brightly. It's easy to become jaded and wearied by it all when you spend too much time on social media – easy to assume that consumerism is everywhere and that everyone is caught up in a cynical attention arms race. That nobody is sincere and that nothing is real, no experience is felt honestly for the sake of the thing itself. But these messages grounded me. There was no phone signal or internet access in that throne room, only the reassuring, solid truths of firelight, pen and paper, and unmediated conversation with other questers and seekers. The people who had come here and felt moved to leave their mark in the bothy book may have gone back into the world to write about their experiences, or make films and package it all up into tweets and Instagram updates, but the experiences themselves had been real. The professional adventurer and the ascetic who seeks no online validation both look up at the same stars – as does the hill farmer who sees the same land in an entirely different way. Wonder is for us all.

Would my anxiety return after I plugged myself back in? I thought that it would, but I felt better equipped to handle it now that I knew myself so much better. And maybe I could reach deep within and bring back an echo of this night at Kearvaig to use as a shield against the overwhelm and the emails and the imposter syndrome. *It's going to be all right,* I wrote on a piece of paper and slipped it between the pages of a book of poetry I found on the shelf. And I believed it.

Later, I went outside to see the bothy hunkered down beneath the blaze of the Milky Way and a million other stars. Never in my life had I seen so many. Only the faintest smudge of light pollution far to the east and south intruded in the spectacle, until a lance of light stabbed through the scene from low on the western horizon and then faded. A few seconds later, it pulsed again. It was the metronomic flash of the Cape Wrath lighthouse keeping its vigil over this place. I thought about John and Angela living out there at the lighthouse, and remembered that solitude is something that we must reach for within ourselves if we want it. But sometimes happiness was only real when shared. Christopher McCandless had been right about that.[2]

'Silence,' said acoustic ecologist Gordon Hempton, 'is not the absence of something but the presence of everything.'

***

---

2 Krakauer, *Into the Wild*

Day 26: 3 March 2019

Last night I'd added up a few statistics about my journey. According to the track logs I'd recorded with my GPS, I'd walked 299 miles from Ardnamurchan Point to Cape Wrath. The missing mile irritated me more than it should have, but it was all arbitrary anyway – I'd walked several miles from the ferry to the lighthouse on that first day, and on this final day I'd be walking many more, because the ferry across the Kyle of Durness didn't run in the winter and I had a hard, pathless slog to look forward to around the estuary's mudflats. Who was to say where the journey began and ended? Did anything truly start or finish?

These were the idle thoughts drifting through my head as I turned a corner in the path and my phone buzzed in my pocket. I'd deactivated airplane mode after leaving the bothy because I knew that I'd find signal again at some point that day, and I wanted to let Hannah know that I had finished the trail safely. There was something else too, of course. At some point I would have to reconnect myself to the internet. I'd put off thinking about that moment because even after all this time I still didn't know how I'd take it. I was looking forward to the feeling of connection, rather than connectivity; I had missed many of my friends and online acquaintances, but I hadn't missed the background hum of everything all at once. I wondered if I would be able to use the web more intentionally now, or if I'd be sucked back into the data maelstrom with scarcely a blip.

It was a system notification:

iPhone not backed up. This iPhone hasn't been backed up in 30 days. Backups happen when this iPhone is connected to power, locked, and on Wi-Fi.

The phone glowed in my hand. A bar of 4G winked at the top of the screen, grew steady. A moment ago this object had just been a flat glassy pebble in my pocket; now it was an infinity pool, a portal into a universe vast and complex and ever-changing. That universe scared me more than a little, but I also missed it. I missed the compression of distance between me and people I loved, missed the Wikipedia voyages of discovery, even missed the feeling of numb immersion in no-time. Not every waking moment can be filled with grace and wonder. We all need a little anaesthesia every now and again.

Even a journey as charged with unexpected magic as this one must come to an end, and when the wonderful becomes everyday it's time to return and face whatever reality you've built for yourself back in the fast lane – but return changed. *Don't forget how to see, how to think, how to feel and touch. Don't forget what is important.* That's what I told myself as I mentally prepared for the shock of re-entry.

I thought about my dad, and how he must have felt returning to shore after a long spell aboard *Yorrel.* Did such existential thoughts bother him, or were the 1970s truly a simpler time? A month ago I'd believed that Dad's isolation out there on the water had been pristine, an ideal no longer attainable in our hyper-connected world, but I'd come to realise that it was an illusion. No generation is immune to stress or anxiety. I had believed that shifting baseline syndrome affected our experience of solitude as surely as it affected our experience of the natural world, but that isn't true: the ability to be still is deep within ourselves, and can be nurtured and strengthened. Our innermost thoughts remain our own, but nature has no hidden wellsprings of power. All is laid bare before the ravenous juggernaut of civilisation.

I wasn't going to stop being wary of anxiety triggers related to my own specific use of technology, but resisting the evils of social media wasn't a hill I planned to die on. Going offline for a month had made me feel more positive about social media, the internet, email, and all the rest. Perhaps it had just given me the breathing space I needed to work out what I really thought.

If I wanted a cause to get behind, it had been right in front of me all the time. The skull at Sandwood Bay had only shown me what I already knew. My energy was needed for a more important fight.

I opened the settings app and reactivated internet access, then I tapped the Safari icon and navigated to Twitter. Within moments of tweeting my announcement that I had completed my journey – my first tweet in over thirty days – the likes, retweets and @ mentions were flooding in, and my first reaction was one of overwhelm: so much information flooding in so quickly, so many colours, so much to scroll through. Then I started focusing on the human beings behind the avatars, and I felt my-self relax. There was a blogger whose work I'd enjoyed for years; there was one of my *TGO* colleagues; there was one of my oldest friends, tell-ing me that she couldn't wait to hear more about my journey. Suddenly the likes weren't just sinister dopamine pings designed to modify my behaviour and rob me of my spare time but actual points of contact with real people.

Another notification, this time from Hannah:

Have you finished the trail, then?xxx

She answered on the second ring.

'I'm back in signal.'

'So I see,' she said, then chuckled. 'I thought you'd ring me first, but you're all over Twitter.'

'Sorry, I'd meant to ring you first, but … '

I trailed off. *But what?* I asked myself. Why had I gone straight on Twit-ter instead of calling my wife? With a nagging sense of unease, I won-dered if a month had been long enough after all, if anything had changed. Maybe it wasn't over yet. Maybe I still had much to learn.

A while later, I called my mum, and I heard her voice light up on the other end of the line. By her tone I could tell that she was having one of her good days.

'Oh, I wondered if you'd finish today! Well done. Yes, I'm feeling much better now, thank you. I can't wait until you're home and you can show me all your pictures. How far have you walked?'

'Up to this point, a bit over three hundred miles,' I told her.

'I'm so glad that you took the satellite tracker,' she said, changing the subject abruptly. 'At times I've felt so depressed while you were away, but I was always able to look at the map and see where you were. It has really helped me to cope. Hannah has been lovely, but you know what

I've been like since Ian went. The tracker made all the difference. It's felt so strange looking at your Twitter and seeing nothing for weeks, as if you weren't there at all.'

I didn't know what to say to that. I wanted to tell her that I relished my separation from the crude, incomplete digital shadows that were nothing more than echoes of my true self in a sterile corporate plane of existence. But my mum didn't have the same hang-ups about technology as I did. Her little Chromebook was a lifeline, enabling her to keep in touch with distant family and friends, and I had never been able to express to her how my experience of technology was so radically different. Now, for the first time, I thought that maybe she had it the right way round – or something closer to it, at least.

'The Machine is much,' E.M. Forster wrote in *The Machine Stops,* 'but it is not everything.'

Epilogue

The moment when our eyes meet is electrifying.

I crouch in the long grass behind the gate, all but buried in the black-thorn hedge to my left. Sparkling early morning light winks through a gap in the hedge as branches breathe in and out, stirred by the lightest breeze, and I try not to move – or perhaps subconsciously I move as one with the hedge stabbing through my jacket, holding me firmly with its thorns. I try not to exhale. Slowly, I raise the camera to my eye, grasping the lens barrel firmly with my left hand as my finger curls over the shutter release. I look through the eyepiece, but I don't squeeze the shutter just yet.

Every morning since late March, when the UK plunged into its long Covid-19 nightmare, I have walked a circuit through a local nature reserve here in the lowlands of Lincolnshire. In a very ordinary landscape I have found a place with such magic, but it does not reveal itself easily. When the light is right and the soul is open, sometimes – just sometimes – I've been privileged to experience the most intense wildlife encounters of my life. A barn owl swooping directly overhead and catching a vole in the meadow by the bridge. A fox watching me from a hole in the hedgerow. The dance and clickety buzz of the sedge warblers. My friend the blackcap, singing so hopefully each morning from the first ash tree I walk beneath. And now, most enthralling of all, this moment that seems to stretch out into infinity until I forget my own name, forget what year it is, forget everything.

The young roe deer hind is lying there in a hollow formed by her body in the long grass. She is so close that I can smell her. Early sun has burnt off the dew in the barn owl's meadow this morning and now soft, diffuse light plays over the green-gold pelt of grassheads and drying stalks that will be hay in a barn somewhere a month from now. The hind is enjoying it while she can. The small animal rolls front and back, side to side in her little hollow, an expression of pure pleasure on her face as the grass brushes her legs. Then she rolls back upright, sneezes, and looks directly into my eyes.

My breath remains held. The animal is no more than three or four metres away from me. I see the textured coppery fur, streaked through with gold and darker hues and giving way to a distinctive peppery mask and moustache-like black halo around her mouth. I see those soft ears held alert and twitching. And I see directly into her eyes: pools of the deepest black, mirroring the landscape all around. I can see the hedge and the outline of the tree behind me and the bright sky above in those curious, calm, unafraid eyes. The universe reflected in this bright spark of a soul in the land of tractors and mud and crows.

She flicks an ear at a fly. I take my photograph, knowing even before I've pressed the shutter that it will be the best wildlife photo I've ever captured. But I also know that the image doesn't matter. In such moments we glimpse immortality, not of the self but of all things. We glimpse the truth of how to live a good life. We also glimpse the horrifying fragility of our world.

An instant later, the hind gets up and unhurriedly pushes through the long grass towards the hedgerow. I complete my walk with a feeling of privilege, of wonder, of gratitude, and also of great sadness. The farmer will come and mow the meadow, the whitethroats will fly south when autumn comes, the new housing development on the edge of the village will be approved, and the barn owl's hunting grounds will contract a little more. Another Lincolnshire wood will be bulldozed and no one but me and a few other oddballs will care.

When I get home, I post my image of the hind on Twitter and Instagram. 'That picture made me cry,' someone I'd never met later tells me in an email. 'Just wanted to say thank you. You don't know how much your daily nature photos mean to me. I'm shielding and haven't been outside since lockdown began. It's so important to be able to stand up for nature and I think the internet has helped us all so much. Thanks again, and do keep posting.'

On my to-do list for this week I'd written *Take another Twitter break?* Now I cross it out and think about heading out for another walk.

Note on the text

This is a true story. Some names have been changed, and conversations lightly edited for narrative purposes. The only area where I've veered further from literal truth is the scene with Seb and Claire at Forest Way Bunkhouse. This scene is a distillation of many other conversations I had with family, friends and colleagues over the course of that year. I'm afraid I didn't catch the names of the people I shared the bunkhouse with that night; we did chat about the Haute Route Pyrenees, though, and someone was reading the issue of *TGO* I'd worked on.

Manifesto

Outdoor activities are increasingly commodified and commercialised. While it's great that more people are enjoying the benefits of exercise and time spent in the mountains, there's a dark side too: greater pressure on the environment, and also a crisis of meaning as we look to social media to validate our experiences. I'm not going to tell you that the way you enjoy the outdoors is wrong or invalid, but if my story resonates with you, if you too feel that something is wrong and you're looking for ways to take back control, I have a few tips that might help.

1. SEEK SILENCE

The world is a noisy place these days. Finding the right kind of silence is becoming more and more difficult, and that's partly because we all carry around infinity machines in our pockets – smartphones that plug us in to everything, all at once. Spend too much time reading the news or browsing Twitter and it can feel like the world is a dystopian wasteland. Connected devices have their place, but I believe that we have the right to unplug. All you have to do to start hearing your own thoughts again is switch off for a while. You don't have to trek to the ends of the earth to do this; all you really need to do is put your phone into airplane mode (which forces you to go offline) and go for a walk in the woods. Make it into a habit. It might feel uncomfortable at first, but the benefits are tremendous.

Taking this a step further, I've found it beneficial to impose a personal rule when I go hiking or backpacking: no social media while I'm actually out there. I don't stop myself from posting when I get home, but I find that the enforced separation between experience and sharing helps to build memory, value and perspective. For me – and I stress that this may not be true for you – witnessing a thing and then immediately Instagramming it cheapens the experience itself.

2. NOTICE MORE

What can you do with this silence you've rediscovered? It's yours, so do with it whatever you want – if that means daydreaming and staring into space, relish it. However, it's also a good opportunity to start no-ticing more about your surroundings. You may have never really seen the dappled light and shade in the park you walk through every morn-ing on the way to work, or the wren's nest hidden in the hedgerow in your back garden. Noticing leads to curiosity and learning. I find that the simple act of focused observation helps to calm my thoughts and bring anxiety under control.

3. CHOOSE CONNECTION, NOT CONNECTIVITY

Tech offers limitless options when it comes to connectivity, but mak-ing genuine connections hasn't grown any easier. There's a big differ-ence between posting a photo on Facebook because you're hungry for likes and doing it to help keep real-world friends and family updated. Of course, human relationships that exist only online can be valuable too, but nurturing those relationships is more rewarding than seeking fake validation from people you've never interacted with on any hon-est level. Likes can be addictive.

4. MAKE A DIFFERENCE

Looking ahead to an uncertain future of economic volatility, threats to online privacy, catastrophic climate change, wildlife loss and more, it's easy to feel powerless and insignificant. I think the key to minimising anxiety at a time like this is to accept that you can't control everything, but that there's almost always some way you can make a difference. The scale of global biodiversity loss may be terrifying, but perhaps there's a local nature reserve near where you live that you'd never noticed before, and maybe they're looking for conservation volunteers. Even if it's just helping to count butterflies once a month, doing something always feels better than doing nothing – and it will make a difference. The more you notice about the wildlife in your local area, the more motivated you'll be to help protect it.

Planning a winter Cape Wrath Trail

Due to the mild conditions in early 2019, my winter Cape Wrath Trail wasn't really a winter journey. People have walked this route in genuine winter conditions, though. Tackling it with snow and ice on the ground is a completely different proposition to the same route in summer conditions (which are usually encountered between roughly April and October). If you are interested in taking on this route, here are a few hints that may be useful.

The route that I took, starting from Ardnamurchan Point, deviated significantly from the standard CWT until Glenfinnan. After this, I stuck to the established variants except for a short section near Torridon.

ABOUT THE TRAIL
Start/finish: Fort William to Cape Wrath lighthouse
Distance: varies depending on route taken; typically 230–250 miles
Maps: Harvey's *Cape Wrath Trail* (South and North)
Guidebook: *Walking the Cape Wrath Trail,* Iain Harper (Cicerone Press)

NECESSARY EXPERIENCE
In summer conditions, the Cape Wrath Trail is the UK's hardest established long-distance backpacking route, requiring a high level of fitness, experience of multi-day hiking in Scotland's mountain landscapes, and navigational skill. Winter takes all that up several notches. Aspirant winter CWTers must be highly accomplished backpackers in all seasons, with

extensive experience of long-distance walking in both summer and winter. Winter mountaineering experience (in Scotland or the Alps) is also essential. This is not a trip to consider if you aren't sure of your skills.

WINTER HAZARDS

Severe weather is the main hazard on the CWT at any time of year, but the weather tends to be worse in winter, with a greater chance of high winds, heavy rain and snow. High winds can make walking in exposed locations hazardous (and much of the CWT is exposed, due to the lack of tree cover). A gale could damage or destroy your tent. Heavy rain leads to swollen rivers and dangerous river crossings, while snow transforms the landscape entirely, hiding paths, complicating navigation and turning simple slopes into areas of potential avalanche risk.

High avalanche risk could make many parts of the CWT significantly more dangerous. Even if the snow is firm and stable, competence with ice axe and crampons is a must in order to safely traverse snow slopes. Finally, don't underestimate the impact of shorter daylight hours, a heavier pack and energy-sapping terrain underfoot – these factors add up to a winter day on the CWT feeling significantly more difficult than a summer one. You'll need more food, more downtime to recover, and you may be more susceptible to fatigue and blisters.

ROUTE CHOICE

There are several established CWT variants, outlined in the Cicerone guide to the trail and illustrated in the Harvey map set. The first major choice is Knoydart or the Great Glen. I would choose Knoydart every time, because it feels more in keeping with the trail's ethos; however, it's also significantly more difficult, with several major river crossings. Further north, the Coulin Pass variant is easier than the wilder route directly through Torridon but, again, correspondingly less spectacular. Winter CWTers may well find that their route choice is dictated by the weather. Even a winter hike by the easiest possible route is still a major achievement.

SUPPLIES

You'll need to carry more supplies than you would in summer, as you will be walking shorter days and burning more calories. To make things even more challenging, some of the shops along the way may be closed or have limited stock. In February 2019, I found resupply options at Fort William (supermarkets and outdoor stores), Glenfinnan (a very small shop at the visitor centre where you can buy snacks), Shiel Bridge (a small petrol station shop with limited expensive supplies), Kinlochewe (two good shops), Ullapool (large supermarket and an outdoor shop) and Kinlochbervie (small supermarket). Stove fuel was available at Fort William, Shiel Bridge, Kinlochewe, Ullapool and Kinlochbervie.

Although I don't think it's worthwhile sending supply parcels ahead on a summer hike, it's definitely worth doing this in winter. If asked in advance, many hotels, bunkhouses and B&Bs will accept supply parcels.

GEAR

If you're experienced enough to consider this route in winter, you'll already know what works for you. It's difficult to strike an acceptable balance between functionality and pack weight in winter. I found my pack too heavy, but I often felt that I'd veered too far in the lightweight direction when it came to waterproof clothing. In sustained hardcore winter conditions my lightweight three-season backpacking shelter would not have been ideal either. The reality is that you will be carrying a very heavy pack no matter what!

One area where I think you can safely go light is winter hardware. In an average winter, you'll need and use ice axe and crampons, but they can be lightweight aluminium models if you're skilled in their use. Snowshoes may or may not be needed, depending on conditions. Ideally, you'll have access to off-trail support in the form of people who can help you swap out gear as conditions change.

Bibliography

SCOTLAND'S MOUNTAIN LANDSCAPE
Knoydart – A History, Denis Rixson (Birlinn, 1999)
Mountaineering in Scotland & Undiscovered Scotland, W.H. Murray (Bâton Wicks, 1997)
The Backpacker's Handbook, Chris Townsend (McGraw-Hill, 2011)
The Living Mountain, Nan Shepherd (Canongate Books, 2011)
Walking the Cape Wrath Trail, Iain Harper (Cicerone Press, 2015)

NATURE AND CONSERVATION
Feral: Rewilding the Land, Sea and Human Life, George Monbiot (Penguin, 2014)
Irreplaceable: The Fight to Save Our Wild Places, Julian Hoffman (Hamish Hamilton, 2019)
Rebirding: Rewilding Britain and its Birds, Benedict Macdonald (Pelagic Publishing, 2019)
The Wild Places, Robert Macfarlane (Granta, 2007)

TECHNOLOGY, ATTENTION, SOLITUDE, MENTAL HEALTH AND RESISTANCE
Digital Minimalism: On Living Better with Less Technology, Cal Newport (Portfolio, 2019)
How to Do Nothing: Resisting the Attention Economy, Jenny Odell (Melville House, 2019)
Into the Wild, Jon Krakauer (Villard, 1996)
Notes on a Nervous Planet, Matt Haig (Canongate Books, 2018)

Silence: In the Age of Noise, Erling Kagge (Penguin Books, 2017)

Ten Arguments for Deleting Your Social Media Accounts Right Now,
   Jaron Lanier (The Bodley Head, 2018)

The Machine Stops, E.M. Forster (*The Oxford and Cambridge Review,*
   November 1909)

*The Shallows: How the internet is changing the way we think, read and
   remember,* Nicholas Carr (Atlantic Books, 2010)

Utopia is Creepy: And Other Provocations, Nicholas Carr (Norton, 2016)

Walden; or, Life in the Woods, Henry David Thoreau (Ticknor and
   Fields, 1854)

You Are Not a Gadget: A Manifesto, Jaron Lanier (Vintage, 2011)

Acknowledgements

My wife, Hannah, has been my rock through all this. She not only bears my mountain-shaped absences with great fortitude but also provides logistical (and emotional) support from home base. I couldn't have done it without her love and unwavering belief in me.

In James Roddie I am fortunate to have a brother who not only understands my weird outdoor obsessions but in many cases shares them. He provided support and companionship, and every time we go out on the hill together I learn more about photography. My pictures will never be as good as his, but I can try. I hope that in recent years I've become better at understanding his own lifelong mental health challenges.

My mum, Anita, encouraged my interest in the great outdoors from an early age, and she's probably been more patient with me through difficult recent years than I deserve. Thank you for everything.

Chris Townsend is someone I'm privileged to call a colleague and a friend, and our days together in Torridon were a highlight of the trail. More generally, without Chris's encouragement and good example my career as an outdoor writer might never have taken off.

Emily Rodway, former editor of *The Great Outdoors,* deserves my thanks for helping to make my winter Cape Wrath Trail possible and for being such a steadfast supporter of my work since my first CWT back in 2015.

John Burns, author of *The Last Hillwalker, Bothy Tales* and other books, is a client who has become a good friend, and his detailed knowledge of Scottish hills and bothies proved invaluable. Thanks also go to John for driving all the way to Durness to give me a lift back to Inverness.

David Lintern is another outdoor writer and editor I'm indebted to, not just for past opportunities he's sent my way but for setting an impeccable example with his own work. David also helped out by providing info and comms support during my CWT.

Sue Fletcher, author of more novels than I can keep track of at this point, was with me at the start of all this, back in our Glen Coe years. Few people have been as steady in their friendship, encouragement and belief.

The Mountain Bothies Association have earnt a mention here for the good work they do in maintaining remote open shelters in such good order. Without the MBA, the Cape Wrath Trail would be a very different experience. Please consider donating at *mountainbothies.org.uk/ make-a-donation/*

The John Muir Trust are a conservation charity who look after many of Scotland's wildest and most beautiful places, including much of Knoydart and Sandwood Bay. Support them at *johnmuirtrust.org/support-us*

Finally, I'd like to thank my readers – especially those of you who have been following my writing from the beginning.